"I WANT to make a mark on my era with my will like a lion with its claw." Was Fascism a product of Mussolini's own ambition, or did it more truly spring from the social unrest in Italy after the Great War? Why were brutal squads of Blackshirts allowed publicly to terrorize innocent citizens, and even to take a hand in government itself?

This book tells of the painful rise and fall of Fascist Italy from the March on Rome in 1922 to the sordid death of *Il Duce* in 1945. It tells how nationalism and firm rule at home appealed to the established groups, many of whom feared a workers' revolution. The author has selected a wide range of primary sources to portray the life in Italy at the time. Using memoirs, diaries and news reports, he explains in authentic detail the workings of the totalitarian dictatorship, its crude ideology, and its ruthless invasion of personal freedom. He discusses the ambiguous position of the crown, army and Church, all of them possible threats to the regime, as well as the secret work of resistance groups inside Italy and abroad, before and during the Second World War. Illustrated throughout with photographs, cartoons and maps, this is a unique study of the greatest crisis in modern Italy.

Italy Under Mussolini

Christopher Leeds

WAYLAND PUBLISHERS · LONDON

In this series

Frontispiece Mussolini the propagandist embracing a small boy

SBN 85340 184 5
Copyright © 1972 by Wayland (Publishers) Ltd
101 Grays Inn Road London WC1
Photoset and printed by BAS Printers Limited, Wallop,
Hampshire

Contents

The Illustrations

BLACK JERSEYS AND BLACK SHIRTS.

Signor Mussolini. "I SOMETIMES WISH *MY* 'ALL BLACKS' WERE ONLY FOOTBALLERS!"

A *Punch* cartoon (1924) illustrating the increasing power of the Fascist
Blackshirts

Germany

France

Switzerland

Austria – Hungary

TYROL

SAVOY
(to France)
1860

KINGDOM

PIEDMONT

Turin

Genoa

LOMBARDY
1859

Magenta
1859

Milan

Solferino
1859

Verona

Custozza
1866

VENETIA
1866

Trieste

Fiume

Venice

R. Po

PARMA
1860

MODENA
1860

ROMAGNA
1860

SAN MARINO
(Ind. Rep.)

MARCHES

Castelfidardo
1860

Dalmatia

Ottoman
Empire

NICE
(to France)
1860

MONACO Independent.
Sardinian Protection
1815-1860.
French Protection since
1861.

TUSCANY
1860

Florence
Capital of Italy
1864-1871

PAPAL
STATES

UMBRIA
1860

Lissa
1866
Austrians destroy
Italian fleet

Lagosta
(Italian until
1919)

Elba

THE
PATRIMONY
1870

Mentana
Garibaldi defeated
by the French
3 November
1867

Adriatic

Corsica
(French)

ROME
Entered by
Italians 1870.
Made Italian Capital
1871

Gaeta
1861

BENEVENTO
(Papal
to1860)

N
A
P
L
E
S

Sea

Entered by Garibaldi
7 September 1860

Naples

Tyrrhenian

SARDINIA

Sea

KINGDOM
OF THE
TWO SICILIES
1860

1852 Cavour, Premier
of Piedmont.
1861 Victor Emmanuel
King of Italy.

Entered by Garibaldi
6 June 1860

Palermo

Aspromonte
Garibaldi captured
29 August 1862

Mediterranean

S I C I L Y

TUNISIA
(Part of OTTOMAN
EMPIRE)

Sea

Dates refer to
Union with Piedmont

Italian gains in 1919

The
UNIFICATION of ITALY
1859 – 1870
with gains of 1919

Miles
0   50   100

A map showing the united states of Italy, including the territory acquired
at the end of the First World War

spirit and will soon come to give you a hand (3)."

Mussolini celebrated the end of the war with the Arditi. He told them: "I defended you when the Philistine was defaming you. I feel some of myself in you, and perhaps you recognize yourselves in me. You represent the admirable, warlike youth of Italy. The flash of your knives and the roar of your grenades will wreak justice on all the wretches who want to hinder the advance of the greater Italy! You shall defend her! We shall defend her together! (4)" From now on a close bond was formed between Mussolini and the Arditi who were his devoted bodyguard.

After the war was over, the Arditi soldiers found it impossible to settle down: "In war-time they had been looked on as heroes, but now they were not wanted, and grew rebellious and bitter. Just as they had once been contemptuous of their brothers in the infantry, for the dullness and discipline of their life in the trenches, so now they poured scorn on democracy . . . on bureaucracy and the rule of law . . . They thirsted for action (5)." Mussolini was to supply it.

Most Italians were annoyed at the terms of the Treaty of *Peace Treaty* Versailles. It had fixed the Tyrolean frontier, submitted some 200,000 Germans to Italian rule, and gave Italy Trieste and most of the Istrian peninsula. But it had not supplied the hoped-for territory in Africa and part of Dalmatia. The Treaty became known as "the mutilated peace" and gave added cause for grievance to the Italians who had fought the war.

In March, 1919, Mussolini formed his first Fascist squads. *First Fascist* Their badge was the rods and axe, the symbols of authority *squads* in ancient Rome. The black uniform of the Arditi became the black shirt of the Fascist. To his highly nationalistic followers, Mussolini made a rousing speech: "I have the impression that the present regime in Italy has failed . . . If the present regime is to be superseded, we must be ready to take its place. For this reason, we are establishing the Fasci . . . that will be ready to rush into the piazzas and cry out, 'The right to the political succession belongs to us because we were the ones who pushed the country into war and led it to victory' (6)."

Soon the squads were in action. After a government ban on *Street fighting* Communist meetings was issued, Communist supporters or-

Opposite The house where Mussolini was born in the village of Predappio

ganized a general strike in protest: "On the 15th April thirty thousand communists assembled in the Milanese arena under red banners (7)." It was an awesome sight and the police and the troops "stood motionless with grounded arms. There was nobody who could face the demonstration, people flew frightened into the houses and shut themselves up in terror behind the shutters (8)."

It was then that the squads appeared, "standing in serried ranks, revolvers in their waistbelts, and in their hands the *manganello*—a short cudgel worn on a strap . . . The first red flag appeared, and behind it the long winding masses of the procession. The next moment the first revolver was fired off, and from the pedestal of the Vittorio Emmanuele monument the little group flung itself over the huge mass like wild wolves rushing upon a sheepfold . . . Crying, lamenting with broken heads and bleeding wounds, the communists fled from the square and disappeared into the narrow streets (9)."

D'Annunzio   The Nationalist poet, Gabriele D'Annunzio, was disillusioned by Italy's failure to obtain territory promised by the Peace Treaty of Versailles. In September, 1919, he seized the Adriatic port of Fiume and held it until the end of 1920 against the authority of the government. Supported by a band of war veterans, he showed that the government could be easily frightened. The Fascists were quick to follow his example.

To many people D'Annunzio represented the real government, for he was "in the eyes of the youth of the middle classes and some of the ex-servicemen, the expression of the patriotic passion of a people that had for some months been made to believe that it was being betrayed and scorned by its allies and robbed of its fair share of the booty won in a war that had cost it half a million lives and a million wounded and disabled men (10)."

Pietro Nenni wrote that: "Without D'Annunzio Fascism would probably never have been more than a relatively unimportant movement (11)." Much of Fascism was copied direct from D'Annunzio's ideas, the revival of Roman glory and the use of the Roman salute are examples. Mussolini also adopted much of D'Annunzio's rousing style of speech.

14

Opposite Front page of *Avanti*: Mussolini became editor of this newspaper in 1912

vedì 2 Aprile 1914

Avanti!

giornale del Partito socialista

a Anno XVIII

giuria milanese ha fatto giustizia: l'"Avanti!", ass

Mussolini with the Nationalist poet, Gabriele D'Annunzio

Early setbacks   The Fascists had little success at first. In the elections in Milan on 16th November, 1919, Mussolini gained only 5,000 votes out of the 270,000 cast, in contrast to the 180,000 for Filippo Turati, the Socialist leader. Mussolini became disillusioned and thought of abandoning politics. Several reasons, however, were soon to change this gloomy situation into triumph; the most important was the economic crisis and the division among his opponents.

Economic crisis   The demobilization of $2\frac{1}{2}$ million soldiers at the end of the First World War caused widespread unemployment and the fall of wages. It was also well-known that some industrialists had made fortunes from the war. The government had promised soldiers land, but ignored their demands after the war. In retaliation, the ex-servicemen, often led by the village priests, occupied the lands of the great estates. Serious disturbances also

Mussolini addressing ex-servicemen in the Roman Forum

occurred in the towns of the industrial North, where, in
September, 1920, 500,000 workers took over the factories in
which they worked. Finally, the crisis was dealt with successfully
by the Liberal Prime Minister, Giovanni Giolitti, who forced
the industrialist employers to accept many of the workers'
demands. Although discontent lessened after this, the upper
classes felt that the root causes of the disturbances had not been
dealt with by the government. They feared a Communist "take-
over" since the Russian Revolution of 1917 was giving people
ideas.

Mussolini was able to handle matters for his own ends. At
first, his programme had seemed directly opposed to the Con-
servatives. He wanted a Republic rather than a monarchy,
and he was anti-clerical and anti-capitalistic. Although he
attacked socialist ideas, he favoured a form of syndicalism, or

1919-*Bolscevismo*-   1923-*Fascismo*-

A Fascist propaganda poster contrasting the miseries of Communism
with the benefits of Fascism

workers' control in industry. Shrewdly calculating that any
coming revolution would not come from the divided and in-
decisive Left, Mussolini now transferred his loyalty from them
to the theories of the Right. His close links with the small but
noisy Nationalist Party and the Arditi veterans provided the
bridge.

Mussolini soon became the spokesman for the disgruntled
industrialists, landowners and soldiers—all of whom were
appalled at the successive governments' weakness in foreign
and domestic affairs after 1918.

Growth of new Parties

Because of the particular political situation in Italy, it was
surprising that the government functioned at all. The workers
had begun to form labour unions and then, newly enfranchised,
flocked into two "mass" parties—the Socialist Party, and the
new Catholic Popular Party (the latter organized by a Sicilian
priest, Don Luigi Sturzo). In the November elections of 1919,
the Socialists gained 1,840,593 votes as against $3\frac{1}{2}$ million for all
the other parties put together. Out of 500 seats, the Socialists

18

won 156, the Popular Party 100. The older ruling groups were shattered as Giolitti in the centre secured 91 seats while the right wing Liberals secured only 23. Thus the success of Parliament depended on the Socialists or the Popular Party providing the centre for a stable governmental coalition. The thing which both parties lacked was internal unity, decisive leadership and resolute policies to achieve.

The Socialists were divided into the moderate reformists and the *massimalists* (revolutionaries). The latter, influenced by Lenin's tactics in the Russian Revolution believed in non-cooperation with other parties and in the violent overthrow of the capitalistic system. They shocked other deputies by walking out of the new Parliament during the King's speech shouting, "Long live the Socialist republic!"

Internal divisions

The powerful socialist bloc gradually split into three parties, the left-wing withdrawing in January, 1921, to form the Italian Communist Party, and the reformist right-wing in October, 1922. The Popular Party suffered similar problems. Their only thread of unity was Catholicism and opposition to the anti-clerical Liberals.

At first the Fascists were concentrated in Milan and a few other cities. The breakthrough came in the rich agricultural provinces of the Po Valley. Many *agrari* (rich landowners and farmers) suffered greatly from the savage boycotts which were imposed by the Socialist Unions. A long agricultural strike in Bologna ended when the government forced a settlement on the dissatisfied agrari. They began to organize their own defence, with many helping to provide funds for uniforms, arms and transport for the squads.

The squads' reign of violence

On 21st November, 1920, during the inauguration of a new Socialist mayor, a nationalist Councillor and war hero, Giordani, was shot dead. His death was made the excuse for a terror campaign by the Fascist squads. One of their supporters gave this account: "We have set fire to eighty offices of the co-operative societies . . . and we have destroyed all the local Socialist head-quarters. Every Saturday evening we carry out punitive expeditions. We have the upper hand . . . The authorities are on our side. They are tired of red flags and Socialist insolence (12)."

19

When asked if fire and armed assaults really restored order, the same Fascist replied, "It's the only way. Talk was getting us nowhere. What we needed was arms, and now we have plenty. Rifles, machine-guns, cars and lorries (13)."

Anti-Fascists were beaten with the manganello club or made to suffer a so-called "baptism" in which Holy Water was replaced by castor oil, taken voluntarily or by force. If resistance was offered, "the rebel, having been reduced to impotence, had his mouth forced open, often by means of a special form of gag . . . In cases of obstinate resistance, recourse was had to the stomach pump, as in hospital. The dose of castor oil was scrupulously proportioned to the obstinacy of the victim and the measure of his treason. On certain occasions petrol, benzine, or sometimes tincture of iodine was added. Serious illness and even death often resulted from such treatment (14)."

Formation of the Fascist Party (1921) Success brought many converts, and Fascism became a mass movement. In the towns, recruits came mainly from the middle classes but in the country districts many unemployed labourers joined because of the Fascists' promise of jobs or small plots of land for them. In November, 1921, the movement was changed into the National Fascist Party (Partito Nazionale Fascista, or P.N.F.) at a congress in Rome. There were now about 2,200 Fascists and 320,000 members.

Among the Fascist leaders a certain type predominated. Many were ex-army officers who were glad of renewed "military" action, especially against the mobs that had insulted and spat upon them in the past. It was reported that: "Fascist squads sprouted wherever there was a Socialist group to give battle to and a former army officer, still imbued with the spirit of adventure that the war had created, to lead them (15)."

Revolutionary tendencies Most leaders had strong revolutionary tendencies. Emilio Lussu, a Sardinian deputy, describes a typical leading local Fascist from Sardinia as "a born revolutionary". He continues: "Once when I was speaking in public he [the Fascist] interrupted me by shouting, 'We want deeds, not words! Long live the revolution!'

"'What revolution?' I asked him.

"'The revolution. If you'll give us a revolution we'll follow you!' At all costs he had to have a revolution. The Fascists promised him one, so he joined them . . . At the head of a squad of youths with drums he used to process solemnly through the streets of the city with the air of a Roman legionary . . .

" 'Who does Mussolini belong to?' he would shout.

" 'To us!' replied the drummers.

" 'And Julius Caesar?'

" 'To us!'

" 'And the Empire?'

" 'To us!'

It was politely pointed out to him that the ancient Romans had no drums, but he continued to employ them and had an imperial eagle with out-spread wings painted on each of them (16)."

Behind this fervour, Mussolini was "little more than a spectator, also hailing in the same group, like a fan encouraging his favourite team at a baseball game (17)."

Fascist violence increased during 1922. In his diary, Italo Balbo, a local boss or "raj"* in Ravenna, tells how he avenged the death of another Fascist who had been killed in a brawl. He announced to the Chief of Police that he would "burn down and destroy the houses of all Socialists in Ravenna if he did not give me within half an hour the means required for transporting the Fascists elsewhere . . . My ostensible reason was that I wanted to get the exasperated Fascists out of the town, in reality I was organizing a 'column of fire' . . . to extend our reprisals throughout the province (18)." A weekend of terrorism which was ignored by the local police and government followed.

What effect had all this on the workers who were bearing the brunt of the violence? The best means of retaliation available to them was a general strike. The Labour Alliance called for one to begin on 31st July and issued this appeal: "It is the duty of all lovers of freedom to break, by the strength of their joint resistance, the reactionary attack, thus defending the conquests of democracy and saving the nation from the abyss into which it would be cast by the madness of dictatorship . . . The government of the country must take a solemn warning from the general strike, so that an end may be made of all violation of civic liberties (19)."

The disastrous strike

* Local leaders were called "raj". This came from the Abyssinian word for chieftain.

From the workers' point of view, the strike was a catastrophe. Its success depended on cooperation between state and workers, but due to a Cabinet crisis there was practically no government in existence, and the workers' response was so poor that the strike had to be abandoned after twenty-four hours.

The main effect of the strike was to give the Fascists an excuse for further violence while posing as defenders of the common good. The Fascist leaders issued this ultimatum: "We give the state forty-eight hours to assert its authority over all its dependents and over those who are endangering the existence of the nation. When this time has elapsed Fascism will claim full liberty of action and will take the place of the state, which will once more have proved its impotence (20)." Nothing could hold them back now. On 3rd August the squads invaded the city hall in Milan and expelled the Socialist Council. Before long they had broken the resistance in Leghorn, the last centre of working-class power in Tuscany.

In less obvious ways Mussolini broke the monarchy's opposition to Fascism which had always been a threat to him because of its command of the armed forces. He did this by renouncing his Republicanism and acting more favourably towards the King and by taking such action he won over many aristocrats to his cause.

The Church's opposition was broken by Mussolini abandoning his anti-clericalism. The new Pope, Pius XI, was elected in February and, like the Liberals, he saw Socialism as a greater threat than Fascism. The Church's support was therefore withdrawn from the Popular Party, and Fascist banners were displayed in churches everywhere.

In May, 1921, Giolitti, the Prime Minister, had allowed Fascist candidates to join the government bloc, in order to gain their support against the Socialist deputies. Mussolini and 314 other Fascist deputies entered Parliament after the new elections. Giolitti hoped that the old pre-war tactics would work, and that Fascism would be absorbed into the system. In pre-war days when numerous parties existed, the buying of votes, which was called transformism, was an acceptable method of forming a government. This was not so now, and Giolitti

1 The Triumph of Violence

IN OCTOBER, 1922, an army of some 20,000 ill-equipped Black-shirts marched on Rome. They could have been dispersed with ease by the Italian Army, but instead their leader, Benito Mussolini, was made Prime Minister. "I want to make a mark on my era with my will like a lion with its claw," he had ex-claimed in Milan in 1914. This he did, and the fantastic personality cult of Fascism finally swept all Italy beneath its spell. With violence and political extremism, Mussolini ruthlessly set up a one-party state, in which he promised glories as great as those of ancient Rome. But in everything Fascism was Mussolini, and with his death it too perished. For the people of Italy, however, the twenty years of its existence had tragic results.

Why did Italy become a Fascist state? To understand the reasons it is necessary to study Italy's weak political system after the country's unification in 1871, as well as Mussolini's eventful career.

Unstable government

The period from 1871 to 1914 was one of acute political instability. Weak leadership, numerous parties, and general unrest among the people caused frequent changes of government. Also bribery and corruption were rife among the parliamentarians who were generally viewed with contempt by the people.

Benito Mussolini was born in July, 1883, at Predappio, a village in Romagna. In early childhood he already showed a strong will, aggressiveness and single-mindedness, which later brought him the premiership of Italy: "He was stubborn and sullen, incapable of true affection even towards his parents and younger brother and sister. Although he early taught himself to

Mussolini's early childhood

9

read, he did not talk much, preferring the use of fists (1)."

In his father's forge, he helped to work the bellows while absorbing revolutionary ideas: "Socialism is an open and violent rebellion against our inhuman state of things," his father said, "It is the knowledge and the light of the world. It is justice coming to an unjust world (2)." Later Mussolini began to read the works of such well-known thinkers as Sorel and Nietzsche, who despised weakness and praised force, and he was greatly influenced by their ideas.

After Mussolini graduated in 1901 he became an elementary school teacher. He disliked this job, however, and soon moved to Switzerland where he lived as a penniless, ill-kempt nomad, taking a succession of jobs. On his return to Italy he joined the extremist wing of the Socialist party. From then on, the driving force of his life became political agitation to provoke a Socialist revolution, with violence as the means of change.

Journalism   In order to spread his ideas Mussolini turned to professional journalism. He became editor of the famous Socialist daily newspaper, *Avanti* (*Forward*) in 1912. During the last year of the First World War the Socialists wanted Italy to remain neutral, but before long Mussolini was agitating for intervention on the side of Britain and France. For this he was sacked from both *Avanti* and the Socialist Party. Undaunted he set about establishing a newspaper of his own, *Il Popolo d'Italia* which eventually became his soap-box for Fascism.

The Arditi   When Italy entered the First World War in 1915, Mussolini joined the armed forces and spent seventeen months in the trenches before being wounded in February, 1917. As he was then no longer able to fight, he returned to his newspaper to spread encouragement for the war effort. He kept in close contact with the "Arditi", the daredevil soldiers who were used as shock troops. The Arditi were picked for their courage in assault and on dangerous exploits, and known for their bravery, brutality and patriotic zeal. Their symbol was a skull and cross-bones. While awaiting demobilization they sent telegrams of support to Mussolini. One from the soldiers of the 27th Storm Battalion said, "Bravo Mussolini! Keep striking hard, by God, for there is a lot of rubbish in our way. We are with you in

10

miscalculated badly. The Fascists had no intention of knuckling under to anybody. The general attitude of many politicians towards Fascism is described by Luigi Sturzo: "Among the Popolari, as among the Liberals and Social-Democrats, the opinion prevailed that they had better collaborate with Mussolini, in the hope that, having once attained power, albeit by methods of revolt, he and his friends would tread the path of law and order for liberty, and in the belief that their presence would preserve continuity in the constitutional life of the Kingdom (21)."

By October, 1922, Mussolini was ready for action. While in Naples on the 24th, he, and his supporters, decided to march on Rome. He prophesied: "Either the government will be given to us or we shall take it, descending upon Rome. It is now a question of days, perhaps of hours (22)." With plans laid for the march, Mussolini hurried back to Milan. This was now far from the centre of operations but close to Switzerland in the event of things going wrong. *The March on Rome (1922)*

Mussolini issued a proclamation which was published in the Italian press: "Fascisti! Italians! The time for determined battle has come! Four years ago the National Army loosed at this season the final offensive, which brought it to victory. Today the army of the Black Shirts takes again possession of that Victory, which has been mutilated, and going directly to Rome brings Victory again to the glory of the Capital . . . Fascism . . . does not march against the police, but against a political class both cowardly and imbecile, which in four long years has not been able to give a Government to the Nation . . . (23)."

On 27th October, Fascist squads occupied public buildings in the North and Central Italy. Columns of Fascists occupied three roads leading to Rome. They were under strict orders to avoid clashes with the Army, although this order was unknown to the government. The four leaders of the march, the *quadrium-virate*, reflected some of the different elements of Fascism. General Emilio Bono was a retired army officer and a Nationalist; Count Cesare de Vecchi was from the conservative landowning class, an ex-army officer and a monarchist; Michele Bianchi, Secretary of the Fascist Party, had been a syndicalist member of the Socialist Party; Italo Balbo was also an ex-army officer. *The Quadriumvirate*

23

What was happening in Rome? The Prime Minister Facta had only just given in his resignation. Now faced with this new crisis he exclaimed very agitatively, "You want a decisive step? Very well then, I'll blow out my brains (24)." However, he did decide to oppose the Fascist threat and announced: "The Council of Ministers has decided to proclaim martial law in all the provinces of the kingdom, as from midnight today, 28th October (25)." But on 29th October the King, Victor Emmanuel III, refused to sign a decree confirming this. He lacked confidence in Facta and feared losing his throne to the ambitious Duke of Aosta who had Fascist backing. His lame words were, "But my cousin, the Duke of Aosta, declared that sedition ceases to be sedition when its aims are the defence of the King and the restoration of order (26)."

Military preparedness Should the King have risked civil war and stood up to Mussolini? Already Fascism has broken government authority in many provinces, but on the other hand, the March on Rome posed no danger in itself. The city was defended by 12,000 men of the regular army, under a loyal commander. Balbo describes Rome in his diary on 28th October: "I find Rome in a state of military preparedness. Armed patrols in the streets, *carabiniere* and Royalist guards occupying the city's strategic points, helmeted troops hauling machine-guns and even a few pieces of artillery into position, barbed wire draped round the Tiber bridges (27)."

General Badoglio, head of the General Staff, summed up the situation: "The army has no desire for a conflict with the Fascists, but should the latter transgress the law, I will undertake to restore order in no time. Five minutes of fire will put an end to the whole thing (28)." In contrast, the Fascist bands were poorly armed and disconcerted at being kept waiting in torrential rain outside Rome.

Mussolini becomes Prime Minister Not a shot was fired. Instead on 29th October, Mussolini received a telegram: "His Majesty the King asks you to come immediately to Rome for he wishes to offer you the responsibility of forming a Ministry (29)."

The same night, Mussolini travelled to Rome by train. On 30th October, surrounded by Blackshirts, dirty with mud and rain, singing and brandishing sticks, he made his way to the

24

A Fascist election poster showing the symbols of the black
shirt and the rod

palace. He wore a tight morning coat, borrowed for the occasion, spats and a black shirt—a blend of tradition and revolution. When presented to the King he said: "Your Majesty must excuse me for wearing a black shirt, but I have just returned from the battle which we had to fight, fortunately without shedding any blood . . . (30)" And thus Mussolini became Prime Minister by constitutional means. The occupation of Rome was the result not the cause of Mussolini's coming to power. But next day the Fascist legions were permitted a victory march through the capital which gave birth to the myth of the Fascist Revolution.

Within twelve hours, Mussolini had organized a Cabinet of fourteen members. Only four of the members were Fascists, but they held key posts. There were also four Nationalists, four members of the Popular Party, two Liberals and two Social Democrats. In his first speech as Premier on 16th November, 1922, Mussolini told the Chamber of Deputies: "I could have abused my victory but I refused to do so . . . I could have transformed this drab, silent hall into a bivouac for my squads . . . Before attaining this position I was asked on all sides for a programme. Alas! It is not programmes that are lacking in Italy, it is the men and the willingness to apply the programmes (31)." Because of his threat to dissolve the Chamber if he was not granted full powers, he was given a vote of confidence 306 to 116, the Socialists and the Communists being the chief opponents. He was also given emergency powers to reform the tax system, achieve economies and to reorganize public services.

The Turin massacre   Mussolini had slipped easily into power, but it was not to everyone's approval. Soon the Fascists felt that a "blood bath" was necessary to strengthen their victory. In December, 1922, several hundred anti-Fascists were beaten and at least twenty murdered in Turin. When Brandimarte, the Fascist raj of Turin, was informed by journalists that only fourteen of the men listed for execution had been found dead, he replied: "The Po will deliver up the remaining bodies, if it chooses, unless they are found in ditches or ravines, or in the brushwood on the hills around Turin—except the two who escaped (32)."

In the face of a tremendous public outcry Mussolini set up a commission of enquiry. Brandimarte was convicted of the

A parade of Fascist soldiers in Rome

murders, but the blame was laid to the Under Secretary of State, De Vecchi, who accepted the responsibility in a public speech. Although the government stated that it would take severe measures to prevent or punish similar acts, little faith was put on the statement when Mussolini dissolved the Turin Commission, and instead of punishing De Vecchi, sent him as governor to Somaliland.

So the Fascists were encouraged to continue their barbarous activities throughout Italy. An amnesty of 23rd December, 1922, in fact wiped out all crimes, including murder which had been committed with a "Fascist aim". Reprisals against the anti-Fascists were so severe that even hardened opponents gave in. One Sardinian cried, "I cannot live in the midst of infamy. I would rather open a vein and bleed to death." When it was pointed out to him, however, that he might be called upon to do

27

just that, he had a change of mind: "Well I'll be quite frank with you. It is impossible to go on like this. You may look on me as the meanest of traitors, but I shall end by going over to Fascism (33)."

The alternatives certainly made life difficult. In a letter to *Avanti*, on 22nd July, 1924, a victim's wife related her own experience: "I lodged a formal complaint. The judge had on his table one of the projectiles, extracted in the autopsy. But it was no good! Or rather, all I got by it was this, that the 'Black Shirts' came to threaten me too, obliging me to leave Turin and give up a business by which I might have gained a livelihood for my children (34)."

The Grand Council

Mussolini now created the Grand Council as a rival advisory body to the Cabinet. All Council members were chosen from top-level Fascists, and their first meeting was held on January, 1923. At this meeting it was decided that the Blackshirt squads should be converted into a national Militia and be financed by the state. They were also to be directly under Mussolini's control, which greatly strengthened his power.

In 1923 the Nationalists and the Fascists united as one party. Mussolini forced the resignation of members of the Popular Party. Some of them, at their National Congress in April, 1923, had urged the end of the "unholy Marriage", which meant participation in the government coalition.

The Acerbo Law (1923)

Not content with only having thirty-five Fascist Party deputies, Mussolini had a new electoral law drafted. The Acerbo Law passed by Parliament in November, 1923, provided that the list of candidates submitted by a party which received the largest number of votes, would automatically obtain two thirds of the seats in the Chamber. The result of this was to give Mussolini sixty-five per cent of the votes—374 seats—in the April elections in 1924.

The elections were far from free. The Fascist Party Militia was on duty inside the polling booths ready to frighten the voters, and the opposition press was subjected to armed raids. "Very few Opposition candidates were allowed to address public meetings, and many were even banned from their constituencies under threat of death (35)." Despite this 2½ million people voted against the government.

Many politicians were also strongly opposed to the government. One person who spoke vigorously against the methods used by the Fascists in the election campaign, was Giacomo Matteotti, the Secretary of the Socialist Party. After a particularly emotional speech to the Chamber of Deputies on 30th May, 1924, Matteotti told his friends: "Now you can prepare my funeral oration (36)." The following day Mussolini in the *Popolo d'Italia* wrote: "Matteotti made a speech of an outrageously provocative nature which should deserve some more concrete reply than the epithet of band of scoundrels (*masnada*) which Signor Fiunta flung at him (37)."

On the afternoon of 10th June, Matteotti was kidnapped in a Rome street. At the hearing of the case at Chieti, on 18th March, 1926, *La Stampa* gave this report: "'It was half past four,' stated a boy of twelve. 'I was playing with my companions. Near us there was a motor car . . . Five people got out of it and began to walk up and down. Suddenly I saw Signor Matteotti come out. One of the men went towards him, and . . . gave him a violent push, making him fall on the ground. Signor Matteotti called out. Then the other four came up and one of them struck him a hard blow in the face. Then they took him by his head and feet and carried him into the car which came past us (38)." Matteotti was soon brutally murdered. It was not until two months later that his body was discovered by dogs buried in a wood twenty-three kilometres from Rome. A rasp was still sticking from his chest.

Matteotti was the most well-known of all those who had died at Fascist hands. His death, which followed directly upon the violence of the recent elections, caused considerable public uproar and a political crisis for Mussolini. He was almost forced to resign: "My position is impossible, no one can remain in power with a corpse under his feet (39)." He despondently told a group of Bologna Fascists: "Matteotti's wife comes here every day to ask for news of her husband. I saw her the first few times, but I haven't the courage to receive her anymore (40)."

Eventually five ex-Arditi Fascists were arrested and im-

Murder of Matteotti

prisoned. The ringleader was one named Dumini, assistant to Cesare Rossi, head of Mussolini's press bureau. It soon became apparent that he was the head of a newly formed special strong-arm squad, the purpose of which was to terrorize anti-Fascist spokesmen. Dumini was well-known for other "heroic" exploits. "At Carrara on 2nd June, 1922, he boxed the ears of a girl who wore a red carnation (the Socialist symbol). Her brother and mother protested. He shot them dead with his revolver. For this offence, needless to say, he was not even arrested (41)." One of the murderers later confessed that Matteotti's last words were, "You may kill me; you will not kill the ideal. My children will be proud of their father. The workers will bless my dead body (42)." His death however, did not affect the Fascist leaders very much. Although Rossi, General de Bono, director of public security, and a number of others were forced to resign, the main culprits were released by a decree of 31st July, 1925. In December, 1925, a court declared the Dumini gang not to be guilty of "premeditated murder". They were therefore "eligible" for reprieve under this free pardon which released all those serving sentences for political crimes, excepting murder and man-slaughter.

In protest at the murder, a group of opposition deputies led by Giovanni Amendola, left the Chamber. They were named the Aventine Secession after a group of politicians who had withdrawn to the Aventine hills above Rome in similar protest centuries before. Amendola demanded the abolition of the Fascist Militia and new elections, but the move was little more than a gesture which it was hoped would force the King into action against the Fascists.

The King merely passed back the buck: "A constitutional king can only intervene at a moment of crisis. It is for you, gentlemen of the Chamber and of the Senate, to act! My turn comes when you have played your part (43)." On being shown the records of those involved in the murder he exclaimed: "This is not my business, but is a matter for the courts (44)." As a last resort, when a deputation of veterans protested about the Fascist crimes, he changed the subject. "My daughter shot two quails today," was his only reply (45).

The Stadium, Rome, one example of the kind of buildings built by the Fascists

All the independent forces, instead of uniting took no action. A possibility arose of an alliance between the Populars and the Socialists, but this was opposed by the Conservative politicians and by the Church. In September Pope Pius XI warned the Popular Party against joining an anti-Fascist Front if it meant cooperating with Socialism.

On 27th December, Amendola published in his paper, *Il Mondo*, Rossi's memorandum admitting his part in Matteotti's murder, and implicating Mussolini in the plot: "Everything that has happened has always happened either through the direct will or through the approval or complicity of the Duce (46)." Amendola felt that, at last, Mussolini would have no choice but to resign.

The direct opposite happened. Fuming over Mussolini's "soft" leadership, Fascist extremists threatened a second revolution. They opposed any idea of his seeking collaboration

31

Overleaf Mussolini and four of his generals during the March on Rome

with his old party, the Socialists, which he had in mind. To bring pressure to bear, a rally of Tuscan Fascists, at Florence on 31st December, declared that loyalty to Mussolini was conditional on his taking "dictatorial action" against all opponents. Thirty Consuls descended on Mussolini to complain about his soft-pedalling with the Liberals.

Mussolini's speech (3rd January, 1925)

Assaulted on all sides Mussolini returned to the attack. Speaking in the Chamber on 3rd January, 1925, he accepted responsibility for Matteotti's death: "I now declare . . . that I assume full political, moral and historical responsibility for all that has happened . . . If Fascism has been nothing more than castor oil and the rubber truncheon, instead of being a proud passion of the best part of Italian youth, then I am to blame! Gentlemen, Italy wants peace, tranquility, calm, in which to work. We shall give her this tranquility and calm, by means of love if possible, but by force if necessary . . . (47)"

On 4th January, 1925, *Il Mondo* warned: "This man Mussolini constitutes a pathological case not foreseen in the constitution . . . Everything is subordinated to his mad ambition . . . Apart from his personal coarseness he is altogether alien to what the English call 'fair play' (48)." It was too late now for the opposition. Within hours Mussolini's government had ceased to be merely a ministry and had become a regime—a permanent dictatorship.

2 *The Fascist State*

AS MUSSOLINI constantly changed his policies to suit his convenience, Fascism had few definite principles. In 1919 he said: "We allow ourselves the luxury of being aristocratic and democratic, reactionary and revolutionary, legalistic and illegalistic, according to the circumstances of place, time and environment in which we are compelled to live and act (49)."

As a result Fascism busied itself with behaviour and attitudes of mind, rather than specific aims. It tried to make everyone tough, warlike and obedient tools of Fascism, and particularly of Mussolini, the Duce. It was primarily a movement of the young and the energetic, and Action was always preferable to the Word.

After January, 1925, Mussolini step by step attempted to control all aspects of the life of the people. Article I of the Labour Charter (21st April, 1927) illustrates this purpose:

"(1) The Italian nation is an organism possessing a purpose, a life and instruments of action superior in power and duration to those possessed by the individuals or groups of individuals who compose it. The nation is a moral, political, and economic unity integrally embodied in the Fascist State (50)."

The decrees of 24th December marked the end of responsible parliamentary government. Now, as the following document states, only the King had the power to dismiss the Prime Minister:

ITALIAN DECREE LAW ON POWERS OF THE HEAD OF GOVERNMENT, 24TH DECEMBER, 1925.

"(2) The Head of the Government, who is Prime Minister

and Secretary of State, is appointed and dismissed by the King, and is responsible to the King for the general policy of the Government.

"(4) The number, constitution, and responsibilities of the Ministers are established by royal decree, upon proposal of the Head of the Government.

"(6) No bill or motion may be placed on the agenda of either of the two Chambers without the consent of the Head of the Government (51)."

Creation of corporations

Fascism started to make specific policies that were linked to syndicalist and corporative ideas in 1922, when Michele Bianchi created corporations within the party. These corporations included representatives of both employers and employees. Later Mussolini defined their role: "The corporation will function on economic ground as the Grand Council and the Militia function on political ground". Their aim was: "the welfare of the Italian people" and the achievement of "that higher social justice which in all ages men have aimed for in their daily struggle for the elementary necessities of life (52)."

Corporatism was a way in which employers and employees might work together through the guidance of the State. It was an alternative to liberalism or socialism which were both considered divisive forces, the former because it encouraged self-interest, the latter because it stimulated class war.

The Vidoni Palace Pact (1925)

By the terms of the Vidoni Palace Pact (October, 1925) the Confindustria "recognizes in the Confederation of Fascist Corporations and its dependent organizations the exclusive right to represent the various labour forces. The Confederation of Fascist Corporations recognizes in the Confederation of Industry and its dependent organizations the exclusive right to represent the industrialists (53)." The rival Socialist and Catholic labour unions were outlawed.

The Labour Charter

In 1926 a Decree Law, which was drafted by Alfredo Roco, the Minister of Justice, banned workers from striking and issued heavy penalties for anyone who broke the law. This was a decisive factor in gaining the support of employers for Fascist labour laws.

A peasant leader tells of one attempt at resisting the law: "I have just had a long talk at Bologna with Mario Bergamo, who is my personal friend as well as being our legal adviser. He went to the prefect and protested against the dissolution of our union and the confiscation of the capital of the co-operatives and disputed the legality of the decree affecting us. He was merely told in reply that our agitation was a disgrace and that the Government is absolutely determined to put an end to it." The Fascists' reply was: "The Fascist unit has issued a formal order that no workman shall be employed who cannot produce the card of the Fascist associations (54)."

The Labour Charter, 21st April, 1927, promised the workers such benefits as social insurance, holidays with pay, and extra compensation for night work. Some of the workers accepted these promises, which were partly designed to take their minds off the loss of the right to strike. The employers accepted the social rights for workers: "The Corporative State considers private enterprise in the domain of production to be the most efficient method and the most advantageous to the interests of the nation (55)."

One ominous clause of the charter indicated that employers would not have a complete choice in deciding whom to employ, and that a Fascist would have first priority.

Not until 1934 were the mixed corporations of employers and employees created. Article X of the relevant law stated: "The corporation is given, within its own field of competence, the power to fix salary scales for the work and economic services of its producers, as well as prices of consumers' goods offered to the public under privileged conditions (56)." *Purpose of corporations*

Twenty-two mixed corporations were set up for various trades and industries. They had few real powers. During the early 1930s Corporatism was the one political topic that could be discussed openly by student groups. Many young people felt this new system might lead to greater freedom and some relaxation of the oppressive nature of the Fascist regime.

Despite all the talk about the merits of the corporative state, the reality was different. There was no equality of power between employers and workers. Workers' organizations suffered from *Corporations' lack of power* rigid control by the Fascist party. Signor Bottai, Under-Secretary at the Ministry of Corporations in 1931, stated that "the trade union is a political instrument of the authorities . . ., the trade union official is essentially a politician, who through his technical and administrative work can and does influence the political opinions of the masses (57)."

In contrast the main body of the employers' organizations, the General Confederation of Industry (Confindustria) was largely self-governing. Big industrialists were able to remain fairly free from the state. They bought their freedom by generous gifts to Fascist Party Funds.

Voting and elections   In 1939 the Corporations ceased to be purely economic in character, and became part of the State's political machinery. The Chamber of Fasces and Corporations replaced the Chamber of Deputies. Fascism saw elected ministers and officials as servants of the State, not its rulers. Democracy was completely despised. Roco said: "The problem of Government will never be solved by trusting in this illusive will of the masses, but must be solved by a careful selection of the 'guiding spirits' (58)."

A new law was passed for future election candidates to be chosen by the labour corporations and other bodies. These bodies were to nominate 800 names, from which the Grand Council would choose 400 to be passed to the electorate for their approval.

The vote was allowed only to the "useful and active elements of the nation"—citizens who were twenty-one years old, or eighteen years provided they were married, or widowers with children. To be eligible they also had to have paid contributions to the corporations or passed other tests. About three million people were excluded from voting. The voters chosen were very unlikely to reject the list as it stood.

The first elections were held on 24th March, 1929, one month after the announcement of the Lateran Pacts (see page 65). The result was $8\frac{1}{2}$ million "yes" votes and about 130,000 "no". The results of this plebiscite in 1934 were even more flattering to the dictatorship as there were about 10 million "yes" votes and only 10,000 "no".

The economy   The Great Depression of 1929–32 meant a fall in production,

Mussolini visiting mothers and children in a provincial town

wages, prices and an increase in unemployment, thereby leaving a way for the state gradually to assume control of a large part of industry. A policy by the government of increased public spending and "public works" programmes helped to overcome the effects of the crisis. State financing of industries increased, particularly of those engaged in war production.

Mussolini believed that "Italy can and must attain a maximum of economic autonomy for peace and above all for war. The whole Italian economy must be directed towards this supreme necessity." His plan for the regulation of the economy was based on the assumption of "the inevitability of war and of our nation being drawn into it (59)."

Italian life was a constant struggle and great publicity was given to numerous celebrated campaigns or economic "battles". One campaign was the "battle of natality" which started in

"Battle of natality"

1927. Its aim was to increase the Italian population to sixty million by 1950. Women were encouraged to have children, and prizes were awarded in each city to the most prolific women. In Rome, on Christmas Eve, 1934, Mussolini gave prizes to mothers from each of the ninety-three provinces who had borne the greatest number of children. There were other inducements: a married man with at least six children was freed from all taxation, whereas a bachelor was subject to a special tax which handicapped him in his career. Despite these incentives, the birthrate fell from 27·5 per thousand in 1927 to 23·4 per thousand in 1934.

In his conversations with Mussolini in 1932 Emil Ludwig, the German academic, said, "I find it difficult to understand why, in a comparatively small and thickly populated country, you lay so much stress upon the multiplication of births (60)." Ludwig described Mussolini's reaction to his comment: "Mussolini suddenly flamed up in wrath. Never before or afterwards did I see him lose his self-command in this way. Speaking twice as fast as usual, he flung his arguments at me like missiles. A reduction in population brings poverty in its train! When the population of Italy was only sixteen millions, the country was poorer than it is today when we have forty-two million inhabitants! (61)"

Mussolini wanted a higher population for reasons of national power, particularly in foreign exploits. He asked the Chamber of Deputies in May, 1927: "What are forty million Italians compared to ninety million Germans and two hundred million Slavs? (62)"

Public works In 1928, Mussolini found that public works could be a cure for the mounting unemployment in Italy. The shortage of living space and dangers of over-population were partly helped by the land reclamation schemes. According to the Government some four million hectares were recovered by October, 1933. The most important and most publicized scheme was the draining of the Pontine marshes. Some 60,000 hectares of marsh land that had once been infected by malaria was transformed into prosperous land, and 75,000 people from the poorer parts of the country were re-settled there.

Mussolini talking to workmen on a building site

Mussolini could not refrain from the use of military jargon when speaking to the people of Littoria, a town in the centre of this region: ". . . once, in order to find work, it was necessary to go beyond the Alps or cross the ocean. Today the land is here, only half an hour away from Rome. It is here that we have waged and shall wage true war operations. This is the war that we prefer (63)."

Huge sums of money were spent by the Fascists on building roads, government buildings, Party headquarters and housing projects. In a speech at the Capital in December, 1925, Mussolini declared: "Within five years Rome must appear as a marvel to the nations of the world; vast, orderly, powerful, as it was in the times of the Augustan Empire (64)." Large-scale demolitions took place in the centre of Rome and were replaced by many new buildings which reflected Mussolini's passion for sheer size.

To reduce Italy's import goods, and so "free the Italian

41

B*

The reclamation of agricultural and building land was included in Mussolini's "public works" programme

Battle of the Grain people from the slavery of foreign bread," Mussolini announced the Battle of the Grain. There were regional competitions in farming output, with gold, silver or bronze stars being awarded to the successful farmers. Mussolini was often photographed at the threshing machines, dancing with peasant girls, and drawing his agricultural labourer's pay. Some success was achieved as in 1932 Italy increased her wheat yield by 12 per cent. In 1933 only 179,805 quintals were imported as against 1,091,866 in the previous year (a quintal = 100 kilograms).

The triumph was celebrated in the Costanzi theatre, Rome. Paolo di Cesare stood before the Duce holding an imposing sheaf of wheat: "I am a simple Italian peasant. I lost my only son in the war, but I am glad that I was able to offer him for my Fatherland. In the name of all the Italian agriculturalists accept from my hands, Duce, this sheaf of wheat. This is the true triumphal banner of Italy (65)."

In his reply Mussolini declared, "Next year give me thirty million cwt. more wheat and I will show you that not merely a piece of bread will fall daily to every Italian but a whole loaf . . .

Will you go on with your work, then Italian labourers?" And the answer was roared back from every side: "We will! We will! (66)"

In the same way the Militia was declared in 1923 to be at the disposal of Mussolini alone, so the Grand Council became his instrument. In 1928 its function was defined:

"(1) The Fascist Grand Council is the supreme organ which co-ordinates and integrates all the activities of the regime that emerged from the Revolution of October, 1922.

"(2) The Head of the Government is by right President of the Grand Council.

"(12) The advice of the Grand Council shall be requested upon all questions of a constitutional character (67)."

Mussolini did not consciously plan to establish Italy as a totalitarian state. In 1919 he had insisted that the Fasci did not wish to become a party or to be tied to any particular programme. Roberto Farinacci, who became Secretary of the Fascist Party on 6th January, 1925, was largely responsible for the Party becoming centralized and increasingly organized on military

The King of Italy and Mussolini inspecting the crops at the experimental grain fields at Ostia near Rome

Mussolini awarding prizes to the winners of the Battle of the Grain

lines. By getting rid of undesirable members he broke the strength of the provincial bosses of the early Fascist movement. The Fascist Party eventually became merged with the government, and therefore lost its separate identity as a party.

CONSTITUTION OF THE NATIONAL FASCIST PARTY, 12TH NOVEMBER, 1932.

"(1) The National Fascist Party is a civil militia under the order of the Leader in the service of the Fascist State.

"(2) The National Fascist Party is composed of Fasci di Combattimento, united in a Federation of Fasci di Combattimento in each province.

"(7) The Secretary of the National Fascist Party, following the general instructions of the Grand Council of Fascism . . . gives instructions for the work of the dependent organizations, reserving to himself the fullest control.

"(11) Federal Secretaries are appointed and removed by the

Mussolini working in the fields with farm labourers

Leader, on proposal of the Secretary of the National Fascist Party. They promote and control the activities of the Fasci di Combattimento of the Province and exercize political control over all the institutions and organizations of the Regime (68)."

The Fascist regime wanted to control all aspects of individual life and leisure activities. Sport was no longer an end in itself, or a matter of personal choice. It became the means for nationalist and military propaganda.

Organization of leisure

One of the aims of the National Fascist Party (P.N.F.), adopted at a Congress in Rome in 1921, was that the Army, schools and various sports organizations "must seek to develop in the bodies and minds of citizens, from childhood on, an aptitude and habit for combat and sacrifice on behalf of the Fatherland (69)."

An Italian Fascist commented: "What was wrong with our working people before the war, was that they used to think and talk too much about politics. They were alright when they were

45

The Duce was very athletic and rode every morning at his summer
residence near Rome·

working, but then their minds were on their work; they were
alright when they were asleep, for then they didn't think at all,
at least consciously. Their leisure hours were a danger-spot for
the whole nation (70)."

The
Dopolavoro

To remove such a "danger-spot" was the main purpose for
which the Dopolavoro was founded. The Dopolavoro (National
Institute for After-Work Activities) was created by decree-law
in May, 1925. All athletic and sports societies, choral societies,
bands, university extension groups, night schools, circulating
libraries, pleasure clubs, with all their property, were brought
under its control. Its ideal was physical training and military
efficiency.

It was the first major Fascist organization in the area of social
welfare. An official publication stated: "The Foundation also
obtains important discounts for the benefit of its members. In
the field of social welfare, the Dopolavoro has created model
houses for its workers, employees and farmers, which fully
answer to the needs of the people. Lastly, of special interest, is
accident insurance which enables the worker to make provision

46

Opposite A Fascist soldier performing an athletic feat

Young Fascists marching past Mussolini (1935)

for himself and his family (71)."

On the tenth anniversary of Fascism, the Dopolavoro had under its control 1,350 theatres, 8,265 libraries, 2,208 dramatic societies, 3,324 brass bands, 2,139 orchestral societies, and a membership of 1,667,000. By 1938 it had provided opportunities for recreation to about three million members.

Sport The control of football players passed in 1926 from local clubs to a central body. They were to be licensed with membership cards, as were 2,700 authorized referees, under the chief referee at Rome, with his gold whistle. A new official, the Commissario di Campo, was sent by the Federal Director to investigate both the behaviour of the public, and any misconduct on the field which might escape the referee.

Eventually, sport became completely controlled by Fascism. Even the Olympic Games committee had to be affiliated with the Party. In February, 1939, the Italian lawn tennis association

The celebration of the seventh anniversary of the March on Rome

said that all players in international matches should wear a Fascist uniform and make the Fascist salute when their opponents offered to shake hands.

In 1933 Primo Carnera became world heavyweight boxing champion. The newspapers were carefully instructed never to show pictures of him being knocked down in the ring. Boxing, said Mussolini, "was an essentially Fascist method of self-expression (72)."

Public spectacles became a popular pastime. The regime made a special feature of anniversaries, with parades, march pasts by the youth organizations and the Militia, trade unions, local authorities and other associations, all in uniform. Flags and colours were flown, bands played and Party and University songs were sung.

Parades and anniversaries

An English visitor recalled one interesting experience: "When a visit was paid to the city by the Prince and Princess of Piedmont,

... well do I remember the loyal proclamations and exhortations that appeared in profusion in the streets. Extracts from one of them I copied into my note-book, because they were so charmingly and floridly unlike the type of official pronouncement I was used to in my native English. It was an exhortation to all good Fascists to assemble in their thousands in the streets of Florence, in welcome of the prince and princess. 'Blackshirts!' it began, 'Our banners flutter beneath the sun of May; hasten, then, with a song upon your lips and a rose in the barrel of your rifle!' (73)"

Balbo's big triumph

On 13th August, 1931, Italo Balbo and his Air squadron received a triumphal welcome back in Rome from their successful trans-Atlantic flight. The Guard of Honour from the Roman garrison was drawn up outside the Arch of Constantine. Balbo reported: "This was the culmination of the Roman triumph which the Duce decreed as a tribute to us. For the first time after a lapse of 2000 years a victorious army had marched along the Triumphal Way ... I had a feeling as I walked along it at the head of my squadron that a great ritual, symbolizing the continuity of the life of ancient Rome was being enacted." He continued: "The troops presented arms. Big guns thundered. The bell of the Capitol pealed in the distance. Then the multitude burst forth with a thunderous volume of applause that reverberated among the seven hills of Rome (74)."

Mussolini rewarded Balbo with the rank of Air-Marshal and made a point of stating that the 12,000 mile flight was really a triumph for Fascism: "You have deserved your triumph for your services to the Revolution, because you wore your black shirts during your expedition, an expedition which was to consecrate in the skies of two continents the solidarity of the Fascist Revolution (75)."

In 1923 Balbo had been responsible for the murder of Dom Minzoni, a priest and leading local Anti-Fascist. During a luncheon given to Balbo in December, 1930, the Lord Mayor read out numerous telegrams of congratulations. Among them was this message: "Unable to participate at your luncheon in the flesh, I am present in spirit. Dom Minzoni (76)."

50

On 28th October, Anniversary of the March on Rome, some

15,000 athletes, led by the Secretary of the Party, marched down the Via de l'Impero. Mussolini and all high-ranking officials were present as twenty-six Olympic champions handed over rifles, each bearing the name of a champion who died in the war or the Revolution, to twenty-six members of the Balilla Youth Organization. In his speech the Duce reminded them: "You athletes of all Italy have particular duties. You must be tenacious, chivalrous, daring. Remember that when you fight beyond our frontiers, to your muscles, and above all to your spirits, is confided at that moment the honour and sporting prestige of the Nation (77)."

Among the many other ceremonies to mark the day, was the distribution by Mussolini of rewards of money to the "Faithful of the Soil". Every two years this institution, which was dedicated to the memory of Mussolini's brother Arnaldo, offered prizes to the contract-workers and *mazzadri*, heads of families who, for more than 100 years, had resided on the same farm, and with their labour had helped produce notable agricultural improvements.

On 29th January, 1929, a circular issued by the Fascist Nationalist Party decreed: "publishing houses are invited to submit the proofs of all works which have a political character or content, to the Fascist federations, in order to permit a close censorship (78)." In addition a list of banned books was circulated to book-dealers.

Signor Ugo Ojetti, the noted theoretician of Fascism, commented in his newspaper: "Reader, let not the small number of books under review amaze you. Ours is an era of action, when not books but deeds matter. Instead of reading superfluous books, read rather—and reread—the speeches of the leaders (79)."

In April, 1929, the members of the first Fascist Academy were announced. Benedetto Croce, the philosopher, and Gugliemo Ferrero, the historian, were not asked, as they were being watched by the police. Signora Deledda, Nobel prize-winner in 1927, was disqualified by her sex and also because she was not a Fascist. The absence of Gabrielle D'Annunzio was the most remarkable. He had replied to Mussolini's invitation with a short note: "A thoroughbred horse should not mix with jackasses. This is not an insult, but an eugenic-artistic fact (80)."

On accepting the presidency, Guglielmo Marconi, inventor of the wireless, said "Italy's soul is growing as its body grows. Arts were never on a high plane. Intellectual freedom never was so prevalent (81)." That month seven university professors were arrested for insisting on academic freedom.

The Academy was instructed to contest every foreign influence in art, especially American films, German architecture, and French literary style. No artistic work was to receive approval unless 100 per cent Italian in style and inspiration.

Customs and habits

In 1926 the Fascists began to alter many of the Italian customs, and one of their first steps was to introduce a Fascist calendar. Mussolini in 1930 said, "The Italian character and mentality must be freed from the crust deposited by the terrible centuries of decadence between 1600 and Napoleon (82)." Two years later he told an audience of doctors, "Our whole way of eating, dressing, working and sleeping, in short all our everyday habits, must be changed (83)."

The first reform was the introduction of the Fascist salute as a greeting. This replaced the handshake and was made compulsory for Party members in 1933, but only in 1937 was its use extended to the masses. In the same year Achile Starace began the monthly issue of instructions for proper Fascist behaviour. These rules were compulsory for all government and party personnel and, as far as possible, for the whole population.

In early 1938 another change was made to an everyday custom. The usual polite form of address, "*lei*" was dropped in favour of "*voi*". The Fascists discovered that "lei" had been introduced to Italy in the eighteenth century when Spain occupied her.

Control on clothing

A control on clothing and style of bathing suits came into operation. Women were banned from wearing trousers. "Hierarchs", the Fascist officials, were ordered not to dress formally by wearing top hats, spats and butterfly collars. Neither were they to be too respectful or over-polite, or to drink excessive quantities of coffee.

A further ridiculous rule was that elderly Party leaders should take part in public gymnastic exercizes. They were made to

A parade of girls wearing Fascist uniforms

scramble up walls and jump through flaming hoops in the Mussolini Forum to keep up youthful appearances.

Even the Italian character was to be changed. The new Fascist man was to be less likeable and more ruthless, serious, efficient, hard and militaristic.

All these rules had little effect on the Italian people's behaviour. They irritated even the keenest of Fascist supporters, and the intrusion into private behaviour was despised by practically everyone.

3 Education and the Church

"YOUTH, YOUTH, Springtime of Beauty ..." sang the young Fascist men. These opening words of the Party's marching anthem were symbolic of their pride in themselves and their youthful movement. Mussolini believed that every Fascist should consider himself a boy as "Youth understands better than old age the two great things in the world: Love and Sacrifice." On one occasion, while speaking to the Senate he said: "Am I blamed for riding on horseback? But I am young! Youth is a divine ailment from which we recover a little with every day that passes! (84)" On seeing an armchair in front of his table, he exclaimed: "An armchair? An armchair for me? Take it away at once, or I shall throw it out the window. Armchairs and slippers are the ruination of mankind (85)."

Fascism and youth

The cult of youth became one of the outstanding features of Fascism. In 1930, Starace, the Secretary of the Party, gave the subject of age pride of place in an order of the day: "The regime is, and intends to remain, a regime of the young, even from the point of view of actual age, wherever it is possible. To give an example: other things being equal, when we have to choose between thirty years of age and forty years of age, we prefer the thirties (86)."

But what of the older man? "In the case of a distinguished recruit to Fascism—a man of real eminence or one who was known for his signal public services; in such a case, no doubt, exception would be made, but not otherwise. Admission to membership was a privilege, not the right of all and sundry (87)." No time was lost in encouraging children to become

55

Opposite A cartoon showing Italy held by three powers, the King, the Pope and Mussolini

Mussolini visiting a school

Fascists—the future power of the party would be in their hands. To this end Fascist education became the means of moulding the total character of the child.

The syllabus and curriculum for schools was repeatedly changed to suit Fascist ideas. Unsuitable books were removed and certain others standardized and made compulsory. Mixed schooling was eventually abolished since male supremacy was a Fascist principle.

Practically all learning was related to Rome and Italy, to the Caesars who had built the past empire, and to Mussolini who was building the present: "In the reader for the fourth form there is given the life of the greatest man who ever lived in Italy, Benito Mussolini, paraphrased like the life of Jesus Christ, from the time of birth in the house of his poor parents in Nazareth Predappio, until that day when his spirit conquers Rome (88)."

Children learned how Italy had won the First World War. Three boys named Sergio, Anselmuccio and Cherubino were told: "It was Italy's entry that decided the fate of the war. For once and for all, boys, you must get this into your heads, and all future generations must get it into theirs: It was Italy that won the war at the Battle of Vittorio Veneto. Say that after me, all three of you . . . (89)"

The compulsory book for eight year olds gave vivid ideas of challenge and obedience: "The eyes of the Duce are on every one of you . . . A child who, even while not refusing to obey, asks 'Why?' is like a bayonet made of milk . . . 'You must obey because you must,' said Mussolini (90)." "Why are you a Balilla? Why are you a 'Little Italian Girl'? It is not enough to have a membership card and the uniform! You must be sincere in heart and educated to Fascism! For example, you must learn to obey. What is the duty of a child? Obedience! The second? Obedience! The third? Obedience! (91)"

The teaching in the school books was helped by the juvenile press, of which the weekly *Il Balilla* was the most striking. The material was vivid Fascist imagery such as this: "When daddy brought home a big photograph of the Duce he hung it there on the wall so that his home and his children should be under the protection of the Tutelary image. The image of a man who is so great and wonderful that, with a word or a sign, he can alter the destiny of his country and raise her to the heights of glory (92)."

"Il Balilla"

Every aspect of education became geared towards producing loyal young Fascists from whom would be selected the future national leaders. An essential part of the training became the conscription of youth into military-style units.

The children of Mussolini's Italy were expected to equal the patriotic zeal of Balilla, a legendary hero. Balilla was the nickname of a small Genoese boy who showed courage in the face of the enemy. In 1746 Genoa suffered under harsh Austrian rule. One day a soldier threatened an unarmed civilian who had refused to help push a small cannon which was stuck in the mud. It was said that Balilla in his dialect had shouted, "Who'll smash 'em?" and picking up a stone had thrown it at the

soldiers. By doing this he had started a nationalistic rebellion.
   The Balilla Youth Organization was created on 13th April, 1926. Its symbols were the rifle and the book. The *Child's Guide to Fascism* stated that, "From the age of eight to the age of fourteen the boy, as a member of the Balilla is trained both physically and morally; on reaching fourteen he passes into

A march past of the Balilla, the Fascist youth movement

the Avanguardisti [corps]; while as a youth of eighteen he can take his place with the Fascist Levy in the ranks of the National Fascist Party. Then the little girls between six and twelve are classed as Piccole Italiane; after that they are Giovane Italiane until the age of eighteen; and at eighteen they also, through the Fascist Levy, can become members of the party (93)."

Boys of the Avanguardisti receiving military training

It was stipulated by the Law that organization of the corps of the Avanguardisti and the Balilla should be on military lines: "They shall march by three. Bodies are formed as follows: Squadron—eleven boys and a leader; Manipulum—three squadrons; Centurium—three manipula; Cohort—three centuria; Legion—three cohorts (94)." The programme aimed to "Teach the young the spirit of discipline and give them: (1) Pre-military training. (2) Physical training through gymnastics and sports. (3) Spiritual and cultural training. (4) Professional and vocational training. (5) Religious teaching (95)."

It was specified in another article that: "Religious instruction shall consist of the teaching of Catholic ethics, Christian doctrine, the Old Testament and the Gospels . . . The form of

Mussolini pinning a medal on a member of the Balilla

worship is that practised by the Roman Catholic Church . . . (96)"

For the girls, the organization served "To prepare worthily for life the future mother of the family of new generations; to make her a perfect mistress of the home, not only in the practical activities of everyday life but also in the affirmation of a spirit profoundly Fascist (97)." Above all, a Fascist must be a good fighter; it was therefore up to the women to see that suitable qualities were encouraged in their children.

Military image   A uniform helped the military image. The Balilla boys "wear their own special or embryo, variety of the uniform proper of the National Militia. The black shirt, of course—the *camica nera*—but with the addition of a blue scarf . . . the legs are bare between socks and field-grey shorts . . . Capped in black . . . the caps are adorned with a tassel; and the get up is completed by white cotton gloves . . . The Avanguardisti . . . sport a uniform more nearly resembling that of the full-blown Black Shirts. In place of the socks and shorts of their juniors they wear puttees [gaiters] and grey knickerbockers, inclining to a plus-four effect. In place of the blue tie they wear a looped white cord reminiscent of the French *fourragère* (98)."

Although membership to the Balilla was voluntary, pressure could be shown by teachers who had a vested interest in a strong Fascist State. The offices of the delegates of the organizations were in the school. In fact "every school had been converted into a sub branch of the Fascist Party. The picture of the Duce and the King and the Crucifix decorate every room. Every school has a flag, run up every day to the singing of the royal anthem and the 'Balilla' song and other Fascist songs. Each class room is named after a Fascist martyr (99)."

There were many advantages at these schools, such as special scholarships and prizes, excursions and cruises at reduced rates, free libraries, and social welfare for working-class children. If a child had a good conduct record it would help in a future career. Laws were later passed to promote and ensure membership of the Balilla. Competition between the Fascists and the Catholic Boy Scouts organizations ended in a law of 1927 stating that only the Balilla should be allowed in cities of less than 20,000

62

population. Fascist strength grew more when Catholic Action groups were denounced in 1931. The climax came in 1937 when the government decided to make membership of the Balilla compulsory, and to include also the eighteen to twenty-one year olds.

The Balilla Oath was taken on joining the organization, or on moving to a higher rank. Usually the Federal Secretary would pronounce the oath: "In the name of God and Italy, I swear to follow the orders of the Duce and to serve the cause of the Fascist revolution with all my might and, if necessary, with my blood (100)." He would then ask "Do you swear it?" and the recruits would shout in unison "I swear it!"

The young Fascist organization which received its first contingent from the Avanguardisti on the anniversary of the Italian victory, on the Piave, 4th November, 1930, was addressed by Mussolini himself: "Fascists, Young Black Shirts! Today you have the great fortune and the supreme privilege of taking the oath to the cause of the Fascist Revolution and the Fatherland. Remember also that Fascism does not promise you honours, or jobs, or rewards, but only duty and fighting (101)."

In passing upwards in the ranks there was a symbolic ceremony. A Blackshirt would give a Young Fascist a rifle, and a Young Fascist would hand a scarf with the colours of Rome to an Avanguardisti. Then the young people would embrace and raise a cheer in the name of the Duce.

On passing the final tests they were enrolled as members of the Fascist Party or as volunteers of the Militia. Their motto was "Believe, obey, fight." They were proud to sing the song Balilla. The prophetic words of the final verse were:

> *We are clouds of seeds,*
> *We are flames of courage*
> *For us the streams sing*
> *For us May shines and sings:*
> *But if one day the battle*
> *Sets Alps and seas aflame,*
> *We shall be the bullets*
> *Of Holy Liberty* (102).

How did the Church regard the take over by the Balilla of her position as teacher, guide and leader of the young? In 1925 the Vatican condemned the "Balilla Catechism" as "a blasphemous parody of the Christian catechism." It was then disclaimed by the authorities as unofficial, although its general theme continued to be used.

The text of the Balilla Creed was: "I believe in Rome the Eternal, the mother of my country, and in Italy her eldest Daughter, who was born in her virginal bosom by the grace of God; who suffered through the barbarian invasions, was crucified and buried; who descended to the grave and was raised from the dead in the nineteenth century, who ascended into Heaven in her glory in 1918 and 1922, who is seated on the right hand of her mother Rome; who for this reason shall come to judge the living and the dead. I believe in the genius of Mussolini, in our Holy Father Fascism, in the communion of its martyrs, in the conversion of Italians, and in the resurrection of the Empire (103)."

In 1931 the Pope condemned the Balilla Oath. He did, however, support the academic oath, which was made compulsory for all professional lecturers. The words were: "I swear allegiance to the King, his royal successors, and the Fascist regime, loyally to observe the Constitution of the realm and the other laws of the State; to teach and fulfil all other academic duties with the purpose of forming active and valiant citizens, devoted to the country and to the Fascist regime (104)."

The reason the Pope gave for accepting the academic oath was that the phrasing "puts on an equal basis the King and his successors, and the Fascist regime; it shows therefore that the expression 'Fascist regime' can and should be accepted as the equivalent of the expression 'Government of the State' (105)."

Catholicism was used by the Fascist leaders to reinforce their own beliefs and serve their own ends. A Mass held at the 1938 Campo Dux began with the Fascist song, *Giovinezza*, and prayers to aid Mussolini's quest for an empire. At the climax of the service fifteen thousand youths drew their bayonets and pointed them towards the sky. The service ended with a prayer to the Duce and the singing of the Balilla anthem. Thus the true meaning of Christianity with its theme of peace and love was completely distorted in the mind of the Young Fascist. He spent more than ninety per cent of his time learning about conquest, ambition and the giving of complete service to the Duce.

How then did the might of the Catholic Church, in Italy its sovereign country, fall under the sway of Fascism? With the unification of Italy in 1870 the power of the papacy had been destroyed. The Pope, however, refused to recognize the new state and expected all Catholics to do the same. The new Fascist regime appealed to the Church because of its stand against Communism, and Liberal ideas.

Thus the Fascist regime was well placed to bring about a reconciliation with the Church. Mussolini sought to further this aim. After 1922 the crucifix and catechism were restored in the elementary schools; Milan's Catholic university was officially recognized; state allowances for priests were increased; Police authorities protected Catholic processions. In return, the Catholic Bishops blessed the banners of the Fascist Party.

The government and the Vatican were anxious to settle the "Roman Question" as relations between them had been under strain since 1870. This was due to the fact that the Pope had been forced to give up his temporal power over Rome and the Papal States when both became incorporated into the new Italian State. Formal negotiations were begun in 1926, and after three years of hard bargaining an agreement was reached. The Lateran Agreement of 11th February, 1929, consisted of two documents—a Treaty and a Concordat. The Treaty was a political settlement which recognized the Papal state to consist of 109 acres of the Vatican and St. Peters. The key feature was summed up in Article 26: "The Holy See declares the 'Roman Question' definitively and irrevocably settled and therefore eliminated; and recognizes the Kingdom of Italy under the dynasty of the House of Savoy with Rome as the Capital of the Italian State. Italy, in turn, recognizes the State of the Vatican under the sovereignty of the Supreme Pontiff (106)."

The second part of the Treaty was financial. The compensation

The Lateran Agreement (1929)

65

that was offered to the Pope in 1870, but never accepted, was now paid—some two billion lire (£30 million).

The third document was a Concordat between the State and the Vatican which confirmed Catholicism as the religion of the State. The Pope was guaranteed freedom of communication with the Bishops and Catholics of the world. On the question of marriage the Church ruled supreme. No divorce could take place without the permission of the Church, and civil marriage was no longer necessary by law. Religious teaching was made compulsory in secondary state schools.

The Lateran Agreement proved to be one of the actions which did most to strengthen the Fascist Government. The peasants, long indifferent to public affairs, flocked to church to pray for the man who had "given back God to Italy and Italy to God."

The Agreement, however, shocked many of the Catholic opponents of Fascism, especially when Pope Pius XI referred to the Duce as "a man . . . whom Providence has caused us to meet." The reconciliation between the government and the Vatican did not please German and Slav minorities. Article 22 of the Concordat stated that: "Ecclesiastics who are not Italian citizens cannot be appointed to benefices. Moreover, the Bishops of the dioceses and the rectors of the parishes must speak Italian (107)." This served to exclude priests in non Italian speaking areas where the mother tongue would serve them better. No account was taken of their Italian citizenship.

Catholic action   The basic difference between the totalitarian aims of Fascism and the authoritarian Catholic Church were revealed in a dispute which came to a head in 1931. It concerned the status of the lay organization Catholic Action. Mussolini was jealous because in many areas it was stronger than his P.N.F. Though Article 43 of the Concordat recognized the independence of Catholic Action, Mussolini wanted to eliminate it, and so accused it of harbouring leaders of the outlawed Popular Party.

All the halls and offices that belonged to Catholic Action were closed down, and its documents removed for the political police to read. Many incidents followed, and the chief sufferers were members of University sections of Catholic Action, who were waylaid and beaten by the Fascist University youth. On 3rd June, Mussolini issued an official condemnation of Catholic Action.

Pope Pius XI, in his encyclical "We have no need" criticized this move. The Catholic Church could not support the efforts of Fascism "to monopolize completely the young, from the tenderest years up to manhood and womanhood, and all for the exclusive advantage of a party, of a regime based on ideology which clearly resolves itself into a true and real pagan worship of the state, which is no less in contrast with the natural rights of the family than it is contradiction to the supernatural rights of the Church ... A conception of the state which makes the young generations belong entirely to it ... cannot be reconciled by a Catholic with the Catholic doctrine nor can it be reconciled with the natural right of the family (108)."

Support of Fascism by the Pope

The Pope reaffirmed his support of Fascism with these words: "We have not said that we wished to condemn the party as such. We have intended to point out and to condemn that much in the programme and in the action of the party which we have seen and have understood to be contrary to Catholic doctrine and the Catholic practice (109)."

To avoid Fascist censorship Cardinal Spellman of New York took several hundred copies of the encyclical by air directly from the Vatican to Paris. The text was published in the overseas press before the Italians read it in *L'Osservatore Romano* on 5th July. The Italian newspaper went on sale five hours earlier than usual and was almost sold out of copies before the Fascist authorities could take action.

A compromise was reached in September, 1931, with the lifting of the ban on Catholic Youth Associations, but the conditions laid down destroyed their previous unity and effectiveness:

A settlement

"(1) Italian Catholic Action is essentially diocesan in character and is under the direct control of the bishops, who in their selection of its lay and clerical officers will choose nobody who has belonged to 'parties averse to the regime'.

Decentralization

"(3) The 'juvenile associations' of Catholic Action will refrain from all athletic and sporting activities, confining themselves to 'educational and recreational functions for purely religious ends' (110)."

What was the future relationship of the Church with the Fascist State to be? This was a question the Pope found difficult to answer. At a secret meeting in the Vatican of all the Cardinals in the Curia (*i.e.* living in the See of Rome) it was suggested that the Lateran Agreement should be denounced. However, the majority of cardinals decided that such a step would do more harm than good.

This "line of least resistance" was also shown by the Church's attitude in foreign affairs. In 1935 many senior members of the Church felt that the Italian agression against the weak state of Abyssinia was a just and holy war—a crusade by the forces of Christian civilization. Cardinal Schuster, Archbishop of Milan, in one sermon hailed the "March on Rome" as having "prepared souls for the redemption of Ethiopia from the bondage of slavery and heresy and for the Christian renewal of the ancient Empire of Rome (111)."

A Catholic newspaper gives this report at the end of a special service for priests who had distinguished themselves in the "Battle of the Grain": "Archbishops and bishops, parish priests and curates leave their seats and surge round him. Acclamation follows acclamation, and prayers to divine Providence to bless the Founder of the Empire mingle with the cry of Duce! Duce! reapeated in unceasing chorus (112)."

Anti-Semitism — Between 1931 and 1938 relations between Mussolini and the Vatican remained comparatively peaceful. A change came with the growth of anti-Semitism. In 1933 Mussolini had poked fun at Nazi Germany's pretensions to racial purity. In February, 1938, a semi-official announcement denied that the Fascist regime had any intentions of persecuting Jews.

But in 1937 Mussolini did, according to Galeazzo Ciano, speak in a hostile way about the Jews: "The Duce let fly at America, country of niggers and Jews, the forces which disintegrate civilization. He wants to write a book, *Europe in 2000*. The races playing an important role will be the Italians, the Germans, the Russians, and the Japanese. Other countries will be destroyed by the acid of Jewish corrosion (113)."

68

In 1938 Fascist Italy drew increasingly close to Nazi Germany. Mussolini agreed to a policy of racism on 14th July, 1938, when a *Manifesto of the Racist Scientists*, written by an anonymous group of university professors, was published in the press: "The Jews represent the only people that have never been assimilated in Italy, and that is because they are made up of non European racial elements, entirely different from the elements that give rise to the Italians (114)." Pope Pius XI attacked this shift towards anti-Semitism. In September he told a group of Belgian pilgrims: "Through Christ and in Christ we are Abraham's descendants. No, it is not possible for Christians to take part in anti-Semitism. Spiritually we are Jews (115)."

In September all foreign Jews were forbidden to settle in Italy. Before this time many Jews who had escaped from the anti-Semitism in Germany came to Italy to settle. Jews were also forbidden to teach in state schools, and were expelled from all academic bodies. Increased pressure from Nazi-inclined elements within the Fascist Party led to the passing on 10th November of the Race Law:

"(1) Marriage between an Italian citizen of the Aryan race and a person belonging to another race is prohibited.

"(8) (a) a person is of the Jewish race if born of parents both of the Jewish race, even if he belongs to a religion other than Jewish; (b) a person is considered to be of the Jewish race if he is born of parents one of whom is of the Jewish race and the other of foreign nationality.

"(9) Membership in the Jewish race must be declared and entered on the public registers.

"(10) Italian citizens of the Jewish race may not (a) render military service in the time of peace or of war; (b) exercise the function of guardian or custodian of minors or disabled persons not of the Jewish race; (c) be proprietors or managers in any capacity of enterprises declared to be related to the defence of the country . . . and of enterprises of any nature employing a hundred or more persons . . .; (d) be proprietors of lands which altogether have an appraised valuation of more than 5,000 lire; (e) be proprietors of urban buildings which altogether have a tax value of 20,000 lire . . .

69

Overleaf Mussolini and Roman Cardinals give the Fascist salute together

4 Public Opinion and Anti-Fascism

THE FASCIST SQUADS were converted into the National Militia in 1923. A private army of Fascists which rivalled the police, the caribineri (royal troops), and the regular armed forces now existed. Its task "with or without the co-operation of the ordinary police forces, is that of rendering impossible any disturbance of the public order . . . (121)" The rule of the squads

The Grand Council had stated that the character of the National Militia "shall be essentially Fascist, having the purpose of protecting the inevitable and inexorable developments of the revolution of October; for which it will preserve its symbols, its insignia, its names consecrated by victorious battles and of the blood given for the Cause (122)." Its organization, like the squads, drew inspiration from the armies of ancient Rome. The regiments were called "legions", the battalions "cohorts", and the companies "centuries". The imperial eagle, with outspread wings, became their banner. However, unofficial bands of squads continued to exist, sometimes attacking known Fascist opponents, or carrying out random acts of terror on the population.

Some Fascists were members of both: "When the Militia is on regular service, or in attendance on official ceremonies, its members wear uniforms. But when they are out to burn, beat and kill, uniforms are left at home. They are then no longer *militi* (members of the Militia) but *squadristi* (members of the squads) (123)." Acts of terror

They had characteristic names like "the Damned", "the Desperadoes", "the Savages", and were joined by other Fascists

73

Overleaf Mussolini leading a parade of Fascist troops

not enrolled in the Militia. They also lived up to their motto "I don't give a damn". While some acted quite independently of the Militia, others worked in co-operation, with the Militia performing the role of a "front" unit. Here is a report of a Militia attack: "When an attack on a single individual is planned, the assailants, as a rule, outnumber him ten to one: and as a further precaution uniformed 'militi' are sent on in advance to search the house and person of the intended victim. Having thus ensured that he is unarmed, the uniformed men withdraw and the 'squad' appears to finish the job (124)." The worst hit areas were outlying suburbs of cities or remote country areas where their methods could be used without causing too much public outcry.

*Squads'
actions
deplored* Officially, the actions of the squads were deplored. Mussolini in 1925 wrote: "It is opportune to state that Fascist armed squads did serve their purpose at the proper moment. They must now cease functioning. They should form a regular part of the Militia, which is the Party's only military formation, as well as the aristocracy of Fascism (125)." In practical terms he did nothing to ensure this. It was only with the regime firmly entrenched that the violence subsided because of lack of opposition.

The Fascist press deplored the actions of the squads. The *Corriere Latino* in January, 1926, stated that "the village Anticoli has been forcibly entered at night and terrorized by a gang of black-shirted hooligans, who have allowed themselves the Sunday sport of a punitive expedition, going the length of pricking with their daggers the unarmed and peaceful customers of a local wine shop. This is an instance of the excesses to which the degeneration of 'squadrism' can lead (126)."

Even the official Militia took part in acts of barbarism, particularly in the Slav and German minority areas of Italy. In the autumn of 1925 the Tyrolean town of Bruneck was the scene of a Fascist orgy: "Nearly all the houses of the town, not excepting the church, had been daubed by the Blackshirts with the tricolours, the badge of the victors' faces, death's-heads and threats. Numbers of townsfolk were struck or beaten in the streets and the ale-houses for no more than speaking German.

Opposite A portrait of Mussolini taken a few hours after his attempted assassination (1925)

'We are here to mete out thrashings', announced the Fascists (127)."

Suppression of opposition After a fourth attempted assassination of the Duce by Tito Zaniboni, formerly a leading socialist in the Chamber of Deputies, on 28th October, 1926, a law was passed to curb all forms of opposition. This gave legality to acts of violence against anything whatsoever that a Fascist wished to term "opposition". The measures proposed for the Defence of the State Act included:

"(1) The cancellation and revision of all passports issued up to date and the taking of the severest action against those who attempt to cross the frontier without a passport.

"(2) The suspension for an indeterminate period of all daily and political newspapers opposed to the Fascist regime.

"(3) The disbandment of all parties, associations and organizations whose acts are opposed to the regime (128)."

Retaliation from the Fascists was to be expected for men like Emilio Lussu, a Sardinian Deputy and an anti-Fascist, who once refused to sign a Fascist document. He describes the experience: "I glanced at the paper. It was a legal document beginning: 'In the name of H.M. Victor Emanuel III, by the Grace of God and the Will of the People, etc., etc.,' There followed a declaration in which I disavowed my political past and recognized Fascism as the only party capable of saving Italy. At the end were the words: 'Read, approved and signed.' I was expected to sign (129)."

He was eventually arrested and sentenced to deportation, ostensibly for having killed in self-defence a Fascist member of a mob which had tried to break into his house.

A Fascist persecution Sarto, a Roman workman, also tells how he was persecuted by the Fascists: "The Fascists wanted me to join the *fascio* or Fascist battalion, of my district. They began by flattering me, pointing out that I had been an *ardito*—a brave and fearless soldier—during the War and that it was my duty to join them . . . When I refused, the persecutions began. My home was searched. During the last ten years I have been arrested hundreds of times, charged with being a conspirator, a dynamiter, a dangerous criminal. Every time, they used to keep me in prison a couple of days and then let me go. In consequence, I wasn't able to work regularly and soon I could no longer find any work at all. People were afraid to employ me because of the suspicion with which the police had surrounded me (130)." In the end, Sarto was deported.

Over the entrance of one Fascist Militia barracks at Magnano-poli was the blatant message "Who enters, dies". Above it was painted a skull and crossbones.

Police measures that had previously applied to criminals were now used against all political opponents of Fascism: "The chief police officer of the district may . . . request the prefect to present an admonition to idlers, habitual vagabonds . . . pimps, vendors of harmful drugs . . . and whoever are singled out by public rumour as being dangerous to the State . . . (131)" "If they are a danger to public safety, the following persons may be assigned to compulsory domicile under police supervision, with an obligation to work:

Decrees on public safety

"(1) Those who have received an admonition (warning);

"(2) Those who have committed or have shown a deliberate intention of committing any act calculated to bring about violent disturbance to the national, social, or economic regulations of the State . . . or to impede the carrying out of the functions of the State in such a manner as to injure in any way the national interests either at home or abroad.

"A sentence of compulsory domicile will last no less than one nor more than five years, and will be carried out either in a colony or a commune of the Kingdom other than the normal residence of the sentenced person (132)."

The men who were sentenced to deportation by the Fascists rarely saw a judge. Many did not even know what the charge against them was. A suspect could be arrested and thrown into prison. Eventually he was deported without having any opportunity to defend himself. One such example was Francesco Nitti, a lawyer, who was considered politically suspect as a nephew of ex-Premier Nitti. The fact that he had twice attempted to place a bunch of flowers on the spot where Matteotti's body was found on the anniversary of his death was enough to send him by "administrative order" to spend five years in exile on the island of Lipari.

An "administrative order"

In 1926 a special Tribunal of the State was set up with power to pass sentence of death or lengthy prison terms for political crimes. It was mainly a military Tribunal, with its members chosen from among high-ranking officers in the army, air force, or party Militia. Originally meant to last five years this highly biased court remained in power until 1941. It was very rare for a person to be acquitted, and even if he was, he would still be deported to a penal settlement.

Until regular courts were finally "Fascistized" in about 1928, fair judgement could still be passed. However, "administrative orders" over-rode many decisions. Filippo Turati, the seventy year old former leader of the Reformist (Right-wing) Socialist Party, despite pleas of ill-health, was refused permission to emigrate. In 1926 two friends, Carlo Roselli and Ferruccio Parri, helped him to escape by motorboat to Corsica. On their return to Italy they were arrested and tried at Savona before a court which still used pre-Fascist procedures. The trial turned into an accusation of Fascism. They were sentenced to only ten months imprisonment. An onlooker reported: "There was a moment's stupefaction, then the truth dawned upon the packed court." The judges "had rejected the Public Prosecutor's charge of political motives, and in so doing, incredible as it may seem to English minds, they had risked their whole careers . . . There was a burst of clapping, shouts of 'Viva, viva.' (133)" Upon their release, however, Roselli and Parri were re-arrested and without new trial banished to Lipari and Ustica.

In many cases ordinary citizens were arrested on trivial charges. They might only have been indiscreet in criticizing the Duce or the regime, but even the most innocent could be caught unawares. One such unfortunate was a peasant pedlar of cloth: "One day trade being bad, the hawker had walked through the streets shouting that he was selling silk muslin at a very cheap price. The word muslin is in Italian *mussolina*, and that simple fact proved his undoing. He was denounced as a propagandist who, under the pretence of ordinary trade, was seeking to bring the name of the Duce into contempt . . . He was imprisoned first in Italy, and later sentenced to deportation to the island of Lipari for five years (134)."

One year in prison was the penalty for anyone found possessing some of the following questions and answers which were being secretly circulated:

"(2) Who is Mussolini?
  He is the eternal father.
"(4) Does Mussolini know everything?
  Mussolini knows everything. He is omniscient.
"(6) For what purpose did Mussolini create you?
  Mussolini has created me to fight the Bolsheviki.
"(7) What are the verities revealed by Mussolini?
  They are comprised in the Credo.
"(9) Recite it.
'I believe in Mussolini, the almighty father, creator of Fascism and the Black Shirts, conceived post-bellum, born of Karl Marx and Gabriele d'Annunzio, came into this world under the Red Flag, was crucified, died and was buried, descended into hell, but on the third day was resurrected with a black-jack [manganello] in his right hand and a bottle of castor oil in his left. He conquered Rome and now sits on the Viminale to judge the quick and the dead' (135)."

"Confino" was the method used to remove anyone who had for some reason displeased any Fascist. The penal settlements were mainly islands such as Ponza, Lipari, Lampedusa and others which were dotted round the coast of Sicily and Sardinia. Most of them were rocky and desolate with an insufficient supply of drinking water. *"Confino"*

Life on the islands was rigorous: "Time for outdoor exercize in the limited zone was carefully regulated. Roll-calls were frequent, at all hours of the day or night, and any breaking of the rules in force was punished by from three to six months in prison ... Every day the prisoners have to be reminded of the power of the Fascist regime. The bugles from the castle sounded Fascist calls; the militia paraded the streets, jeering at the impotent political adversaries of the Government (136)."

On 1st December, 1930, the daily maintenance allowance was reduced from about 10p to 5p a day. Few of the deportees received regular aid from their families as most of them were poor workmen. Emilio Lussu wrote: "So small a sum was

81

hopelessly inadequate for the necessities of life, and economy became a fine art among the deportees; but, even so, privation was universal and the diseases of privation, especially tuberculosis and dysentry, were consequently widespread (137)."

Upon arrival on an island every deportee received a residence permit (*carta di permanenza*) on which was printed the rules, some examples were:

"(1) To take regular work in respect of which this office must be notified.

"(2) Not to leave the allotted dormitory or dwelling, or to go without permission beyond certain limits.

"(3) To return to the dormitory in the evening at sunset, or earlier if the office so orders; not to leave it before the hour of opening.

"(5) Not to frequent brothels, and not to frequent cafes, inns or public houses and indulge in dissipation.

"(6) Not to attend public meetings, processions, plays or public entertainments.

"(8) To be of good conduct, and give no cause for suspicion.

"(10) Always to carry this card and to present it on request (138)."

Punishments for deportees The punishments for deportees were invariably severe. In *Escape*, Francesco Fausto Nitti describes a Lieutenant Veronica, who was eventually relieved of his duties and considered mad, because of his brutality towards the deportees at Lampedusa.

The smallest pretext could be used as an excuse for violence. Once Lieutenant Veronica shouted, "It is impossible to argue with you people. You are all too cultured and educated! I, for my part, am going to propose another method of settling our differences of opinion. Let's both go out into a field outside the village. I'll take off my uniform of an officer of the Fascist militia and we'll fight it out with our fists. Are you willing? I'm just longing to push your face in." On another occasion he shouted, "Here is Fascism", brandishing his whip, "this is our power, our strength, our argument! This and only this shall I use in future (139)."

Censorship of correspondence The political prisoner had no rights of any kind. His mail, even, did not belong to him. "Letters coming to interned persons were always opened, censored, and often confiscated, while those who corresponded with them had their names added to the list of political suspects, and so endangered their own freedom . . . To send letters except through the police was to risk imprisonment of up to six months (140)."

Nitti tells how he was questioned about a list of names found on him when arrested. " 'Who are these people? They appear to be freemasons.' 'Oh no, Lieutenant, they are Protestants. They have nothing to do with politics . . .' 'Very well, I understand. I shall transmit these addresses to Rome immediately. We'll teach these gentlemen to protest! They are all cowards and rogues' (141)."

In contrast to the brutality shown to the opponents of the State, there was also the "kid-glove" treatment to Fascists who committed illegal acts. "If by some chance a Fascist is found guilty of any crime which can possibly be classed as political, he may be sure that the prison doors will soon be opened by means of a special pardon or a general amnesty (142)." Two amnesties before August, 1925, wiped off the slate all political crimes, except murder. *Fascist crimes excused*

How could Fascism justify these double standards? "The official theory of the Fascist Party is that political crimes committed by its members are revolutionary acts not to be judged by the ordinary standards of right and wrong (143)." Mussolini supported this view in *Gerachia*, the official Fascist journal, in October, 1925. "Violence is moral, provided it is timely and surgical and chivalrous . . . Private and individual ungoverned violence is anti-Fascist . . . The Italian people understand the use of governmental violence in certain contingencies through the regular armed forces, but not supplemental individual violence (144)."

Thus it was that the police and magistrates worked on the supposition that certain acts of violence and reprisal were "authorized" and others not.

Occasionally an examining magistrate would dare to issue a warrant against a Fascist: "The Bench of Milan had the courage to accuse before the Chamber of Deputies . . . a former General Secretary of the Fascist Party [Giunta] on a charge of having

83

given orders for the bludgeoning of Signor Forni ... The Chamber refused to authorize the prosecution. The president of the Milan Bench, one of the public prosecutors, and two judges were transferred to another city (145)."

The defenders of anyone regarded as anti-Fascist placed themselves at risk: "On 3rd May, 1926, the case was heard at Mantua of a Communist, Achille Pepe, who had already spent five months in prison awaiting trial. The accused was acquitted of the charge of criminal conspiracy, but received six months' imprisonment for inciting to class hatred. As the defending counsel, Signor Buffoni, a member of Parliament left the court, a crowd of Fascists overwhelmed him with insults and threats. The matter seemed over for the moment, but on reaching the station to take his train for Milan, he found the same crowd of assailants awaiting him. He was beaten and wounded ... It would be naive to ask whether the assailants were ever brought to justice ... (146)"

In January and February, 1926, a prominent anti-Fascist, Gaetano Salvemini, was threatened with death: "For Salvemini there is only one solution: an infamous death. No one need be surprised if some Fascist of heart and courage would lose patience and send him to reflect in a calmer and more peaceful world (147)."

If the Fascist press was outspoken, so too were the writers, editors and publishers of the anti-Fascist press. The difference was that they were forced to pay, often with their lives. Most prominent among the anti-Fascists was Giovanni Amendola, the editor of *Il Mondo*, who subsequently died as the result of injuries received in three savage assaults. His death, which was less than two years after that of Matteotti, deprived the opposition of its principle spokesman and leader.

Mussolini made it his business to hound such men personally. Of Piero Gobetti, the founder and editor of *Rivoluzione Liberale* in Turin, he said in a telegram to the Prefect of Turin in March, 1924: "I hear that Gobetti who was recently in Paris, is now in Sicily. Please keep me informed, and be vigilant in making life difficult again for this stupid opponent of the Government and of Fascism (148)." Gobetti died of influenza after fleeing to

Paris, leaving a wife and new born baby behind. Giuseppe Donati, editor of the Christian Democrat *Il Popolo* was forced into exile in June, 1925, after having been subjected to constant death threats.

To make persecution even more effective, Mussolini obtained from all anti-Fascist newspaper publishers a list of the names and addresses of their subscribers. The list was then forwarded to the local Fascist heads, and the readers of the "subversive" papers dealt with.

With the elimination of the free press, journalism became, in the words of Mussolini, "instead of a trade, a vocation òr a mission". The interest of the nation was to take precedence over the right of freedom of speech. Mussolini's first official statement on the role of the Fascist press was made to the Senate on 27th November, 1922: "Gentlemen, I have no fetishes, and when the interests of the nation are at stake, I don't even have the fetish of freedom. This is why, after some people have talked to me about freedom of the press, I, who am a journalist, I have said that freedom is not only a right, it is also a duty (149)."

The writer, Francesco Nitti, noted: "Mussolini himself appoints or dismisses the editors of the great newspapers, as the fancy takes him. In order to find work on a newspaper, journalists must be *persona grata* with the Fascist authorities (150)." In 1926 the owners of the *Corriere della Sera*, the Crespi family of Milan, were persuaded to dismiss liberals such as the Albertini brothers from its editorship and to ban writers such as Benedetto Croce. A new editor was appointed by Mussolini.

Special decrees in 1923–4 and 1928 brought journalism fully under Government control. No one could practice journalism unless he was approved and placed on the Professional Roll of Journalists. Article II of the 1923–4 decrees authorized the Prefects to issue a warning to the managing editor "if the newspaper or other publication with false or tendentious news hampers the diplomatic action of the government in its relations with other powers or damages national prestige within Italy or abroad or arouses unjustified alarm among the population or causes a disturbance of public order (151)." If the warning was ignored "the newspapers or other writings published in illegal defiance of the regulations in Article II are to be confiscated (152)."

The consequence of all this was that Italian newspapers all said the same thing and thus lacked interest. "They rarely mentioned the king, but there are always three or four columns . . . about the Duce, his great achievements and incomparable genius. Pictures show him on foot, on horseback, in air-planes, automobiles and warships, in military uniform, and even in the garb of a Roman emperor . . . No cinema star has ever had more pictorial publicity (153)." Needless to say, it was more than anyone's life was worth to mention his lack of stature, his ulcer or the time he fell off his horse!

The anti-Fascist press was eventually forced underground. "The Italia Libera" Circle, which was formed in Florence in 1924, issued manifestos denouncing the Fascist regime. In January, 1925, it produced the first underground newspaper *Non Mollare* (*Don't give in*) which urged the Italian people "to resist those who constantly attempt to intimidate us with threats of violence, who buy off witnesses and judges to condemn us, who burn our meeting places, who confiscate our newspapers. It is necessary to resist despite the guns of the police, despite the pardons granted to criminals, despite all the decrees that can be signed by the King (154)."

The "Italia Libera" circle

Nearly all the leading figures of "Italia Libera" paid dearly for their anti-Fascist activities; several were either assassinated, beaten, or had their houses ransacked. Many were arrested and deported.

Between 1924 and 1926 many prominent anti-Fascists escaped into exile. Before 1927 this was relatively easy as the Italian frontiers were lightly guarded. Later these illegal exits became more difficult.

Arturo Labriola, a prominent Italian politician, describes his own departure: "I asked Mussolini to give me a passport. He refused it. Then I decided to organize an 'illegal' flight, despite the risk of imprisonment and a fine of 20,000 lira [approx. £20]. My escape was not easy. I was for five days at sea in a little fishing boat which some trusty men, in danger of their lives, sailed first to Sardinian and then to Corsican waters. I landed on the Corsican coast at night and barely escaped drowning in a marsh (155)." He was solemnly saluted by the French coastguards on presenting his ministerial passport.

"Out of sight, out of mind" was not the case as far as Mussolini was concerned, and he took steps to see that they should not escape punishment. Article V of the Law for Public Safety, 25th November, 1926, stated: "Any citizen who outside the national territory, spreads or in any way communicates false, exaggerated, or tendentious rumours or information regarding the internal condition of the state in such a manner as to lessen the credit or prestige of the state abroad, or who practices actions of any kind that tend to prejudice the national interests, is liable to imprisonment ranging from five to fifteen years, and permanent exclusion from public office (156)." He was also liable to loss of citizenship and confiscation of property. *Anti-Fascists abroad*

Among the *fuorusciti*, or outsiders, were some very famous Italians, including ex-premier Francesco Nitti. There were the Socialist leaders Filippo Turati and Pietro Nenni; the First Party Secretary of the Popolari, Don Sturzo; the Republican Count Sforza; the Liberal Socialist Carlo Roselli; the Communist Palmiro Togliatti; the historian Gaetano Salvemini; the physicist Enrico Fermi and the famous conductor Arturo Toscanini. *The "outsiders"*

Here is how one exile described existence abroad: "Life in exile was hard for those who wanted to maintain their independence. The labourers and craftsmen sometimes found work but for the intellectuals this was almost impossible . . . Tarchiaini, a former sub-editor on the *Corriere della Sera* did not manage to get a single article published and was reduced to such straits that he walked about Paris to save Metro fares and had to share a single tangerine with three other members of his family (157)."

To further persecute anti-Fascists Mussolini formed a secret political police organization, the O.V.R.A., in 1926. The name of the organization was meaningless, and it was invented by Mussolini only to frighten people. Branches were attached to each Division of the Militia, and it was an easy means by which Fascism could enter into peoples' private lives. Emilio Lussu's wife describes their experiences in Paris: "We often had to move house. The O.V.R.A. showed great efficiency in discovering Emilio's whereabouts and each time they found out his address we had to move on (158)."

The Justice and Liberty movement began in 1929. It was founded by Roselli, and "was the first manifestation of definite action on the part of those democratic anti-Fascists who believe that in the fight against Fascism it is useless to rely upon the King, or foreign nations . . . to sweep away the present dictatorship (159)."

The movements' programme was printed on the first page of its leaflets. Certain extracts stated: "Justice and Freedom struggles for overthrowing the Fascist dictatorship and the victory of a free, democratic republican regime . . . It issues a call to action to all Italians whose dignity has been offended by the present state of servitude and who are prepared to take an active part in the revolt (160)."

Its members had contempt for the Monarchy, the Vatican and all groups who failed to oppose Fascism vigorously. In common with many political movements that were composed mainly of individualists and intellectuals, there were strong disagreements and varying viewpoints among them. Generally, members agreed on one thing, that they were against Fascism, but there was no common aim for combating it.

Another exile gave this description of the Italian Socialists: "The communists formed a group by themselves with party officials on Stalinist lines. They received help from Russia and from the European Communist parties, had special rules governing internal relationships and a noticeable absence of external contact. The Socialists all seemed . . . to be old even those who were anagraphically young . . . and to be lacking in revolutionary capacity. Their resistance against Fascism appeared only to be moral and political . . . (161)"

In a manifesto in 1935 Roselli appealed to the workers, "to the young Italians who though wearing the Fascist uniform, feel the stirrings of a higher life. We have faith in that unknown Italy taking shape in silence, rising out of the tyranny of dictatorship (162)."

Roselli's actions provoked Mussolini's intense anger and close watch was kept on him in Paris. When Mussolini intervened in the Spanish Civil War on the side of General Franco, Roselli went to Spain to fight for the Republic, as did five thousand other Italian anti-Fascists. Roselli's password was "Today in Spain, tomorrow in Italy". This was too much for Mussolini. When Roselli returned to France he and his brother Nello were shortly afterwards assassinated by Mussolini's hirelings.

The Justice and Liberty movement also gave support to Fernando De Rosa, who attempted to assassinate Crown Prince Humbert in Belgium in October, 1929. At his trial, De Rosa deliberately accused himself. He wished to die as a martyr of the anti-Fascists: "I wanted to kill the hereditary prince of a reigning house that has killed freedom in my country. I felt that when this young prince behaved like a Fascist ... put on the Fascist uniform, was openly identifying himself with the assassins of Giacomo Matteotti ... I wanted to do justice (163)." The court sentenced De Rosa to five years imprisonment.

Lauro de Bosis, a poet and dramatist, founded the "Alleanza Nazionale", a liberal monarchical movement, in France. On 3rd October, 1931, he flew from Marseilles to Rome to scatter from the air pamphlets to remind Italians of their lost liberties. Along with the pamphlets he threw copies of a book by Bolton King entitled *Fascism in Italy*, in an attempt to counteract those "doctored" versions of history supplied to the people by Mussolini. He commented: "As one throws bread on a starving city, one must throw history books on Rome (164)."

Lauro de Bosis

Unfortunately de Bosis did not return from the journey; although he did achieve his objective. Ruth Draper, his fiancée, collected some eyewitness accounts of the final stages of the flight: "He flew very low over the streets, and in places, it seemed as if snow had fallen, so thickly were the leaflets strewn. He dropped them into the laps of the spectators at an open-air cinema, and among the tables of the cafes in the squares ... There have been many rumours as to his fate but no trace of his plane was ever found. How he died was never known (165)." Within a few months the O.V.R.A. retaliated by tracking down and arresting friends of the Justice and Freedom group in

Milan, Turin and Rome.

The "Anti-
Fascist
Concentration"
What was the success of the Italian anti-Fascist movement abroad? Apart from the individual actions of brave men it failed. The "Concentrazione Antifascista", the largest union of the opposition parties, had its headquarters in Paris and lasted only ten years because of the differences among the opposition groups and the increasing success of Fascism. At best, it had been an information centre and a reminder to the rest of the world that there were exiled non-Communist Italians who were opposed to Fascism. Neither the Communists nor the Populists joined the union and no support came from other countries for their actions.

The Mafia
A clash between Mussolini and the Mafia (the gangster organization) was inevitable. Fascist officials who were sent to replace the old corrupt Mafia-controlled officials, were ignored, and Fascist courts that tried to obtain convictions against members of the Mafia found it impossible to gain witnesses. One report said: "In Palermo a member of the Party could be shot dead at midday, in the middle of the crowded via Maqueda, in the sight of hundreds of people, without a single person being ready to admit to the police they had even heard the shot (166)." The cudgels-and-castor-oil methods the squadrists had used so successfully in northern Italy failed in Sicily against the ancient Mafia defence of silence and vengeance.

The Mafia was in complete charge of the Sicilian electoral machine, and at one time violence in Sicily was ten times higher than in any other part of Italy. Mussolini realized the extent of the Mafia's power when he found himself being escorted in Sicily by Don Ciccio, a Mafia leader: "It was then that the Duce at least realized that things had reached such a pass in Sicily that even his own chief of police had thought it advisable to place him, the head of the government, under Mafia protection (167)."

Breaking-up
the Mafia
Cesare Mori, Mussolini's Chief of Police, carried out the action to break up the Mafia. On hearing that many ambushes took place from behind high walls, he ordered that every wall in Sicily be reduced to three feet within twenty-four hours. Some entire villages were surrounded by the Fascist militia and all

Mussolini on the balcony of the Palazzo Venezia

the male inhabitants over fifteen years transported to prison. One, when asked what he was charged with, replied "I don't know. All I know is that another prisoner, a young man like myself, was informed a few days ago that he was charged with a crime committed in 1908. At that time he was only a year old (168)."

In 1927 Mussolini declared that the war against the Mafia had been won. But it was only a temporary lull. Self protection, self help and non-co-operation were too deeply engrained in the Italian people. Many members of the Mafia emigrated to the U.S.A. where they made illegal fortunes—much of which was returned to their families in Sicily. As for the others: "When the Sicilians hear of the so-called Fascist triumph over the Mafia they laugh. It was well known that most of the genuine members of the Mafia joined the Black Shirts. They even helped to carry out the raids whose victims were innocent peasants (169)."

Minority groups What of the other groups, the minorities, who had reason to hate Mussolini? A certain amount of active resistance came from the Germans, Slovenes and South Tyrolese which the Peace settlement after World War One had brought in substantial numbers of people into Italy. The Fascists tried the harsh policy of "Italianizing" these people by modifying their surnames and interfering with their cultural, religious and educational patterns. The tough South Tyrolese were more successful than the Slavs in protecting their rights.

The Fascists' Special Tribunal condemned, between February 1927 and July, 1932, some 106 Slavs to a total of 1,124 years of imprisonment. The decrees of 8th August, 1923, made it an offence to refer publicly to "das heilige Land Tirol". The German speaking inhabitants were obliged to call it "Venezia Tridentina", and it was punishable not to use the Italian names, even if they had to be newly invented. The writer, Reut Nicolussi, recalls "An inn in St. Ulrich was punished by being officially closed because an iron pot marked Heisses Wasser had been discovered in the kitchen (170)."

The Fascist paper *Piccolo Posto* wrote, "Germanism must be rooted out of the very soul ... this province must become Italian, its inhabitants Italian, so that all therein is Italian, and

Italy only recalled in it (171)." The Germans had proclaimed in 1919: "We are not Italian, do not wish to be numbered among them, and will never in the future become Italians! . . . May the destiny of German Tyrol be likewise our destiny, its future be our future (172)." In October, 1922, the squads over-ran Bolzano (Bozen) in Northern Italy and behaved brutally to the former Austrian population.

The Italian language was made compulsory in the law courts and in the schools: "In numerous places German-speaking parents allowed their children, after duly attending the national schools with their incomprehensible Italian instructions, to spend their free time in learning to read and write German (173)." The Italian authorities threatened violence and imprisonment for all taking part in these "catacomb" schools. "If you do not give up teaching German" a burgomaster said to one woman teacher, "we can treat you as we will!" As a result the "teachers and children could only protect themselves by sentry outposts, secret doors contrived in walls, hiding in cellars, barns or stables (174)."

Italian language made compulsory

Fascism never did penetrate to the roots of Italian society. It was tolerable because it tended to be more satisfied by appearances than reality. Although the state was proclaimed "totalitarian" it did not, in fact, achieve its aim of controlling all aspects of public and private life, and most people still kept considerable independence. It had to compromise with traditional forces. Various groups were neutralized, never destroyed or absorbed. These included the monarchy, which attracted loyalty from the upper classes, the military, the landowners, the industrialists and the Vatican.

Public attitude to Fascism

As all independent methods of free expression had been savagely suppressed after 1925, an accurate assessment of public opinion towards Fascism is difficult.

Even the most enthusiastic support was not all it appeared to be. One Englishman gave this account in 1931 "the crowds which cheered Mussolini's speeches in Tuscany and Lombardy last summer are quoted as evidence of his popularity among the masses; the reports did not mention that fifteen trainloads of Blackshirts followed him to swell and overawe the crowd, that

DVCE
DVCE
DVCE
DVCE
DVCE
11

workshops were closed and the men driven to his meetings under pain of dismissal, that his arrival at each town was preluded by the arrest of suspects by the hundred (175)."

The vast crowds that filled the Piazza Venezia during many of his appearances on the famous balcony were ensured by the closing of all Government offices, and making attendance compulsory for all civil servants. It is clear that the year of 1929 was a high point in the popularity of the regime, after the signing of the Lateran Agreement. Other good years were 1936 after the Abyssinian war, and 1938 when Mussolini played an important part in preventing world war.

During the late 1920s Fascism was accepted widely by the people who were pleased that it provided ordered rule and an end to class conflict. Many joined the Party realizing it offered special advantages, such as better access to employment, insurance and welfare benefits, which were especially appreciated during the rigours of economic depression. The numerous colourful street parades and anniversaries gave many people opportunities to enter into national self-admiration. *Acceptance of Fascism*

Industrialists enjoyed preferential treatment, and more respect was shown towards their requests than towards the workers. Many workers and peasants were never reconciled to Fascism, but because they were ill-prepared to face a life in exile, they bided their time.

During the late 1930s open criticism of the Fascist regime became evident. People resented the increased interference in private life. They also resented the anti-Semitic laws and the close. ties which Mussolini insisted on having with Hitler. The wealthy and industrial classes became irritated by the extravagance and bureaucracy of Fascism. Formerly it had been welcomed for its efficiency and ability to deal with strikes, but now it seemed only corrupt and inefficient. *Criticism of Fascist regime*

By 1939 most Italians were utterly fed up with Mussolini and Fascism, although unable to find any way of overthrowing the government. It was left to confirmed opponents of Mussolini in exile to take the lead in organizing resistance and linking up with partisan bands during the Second World War.

Opposite Striking Mussolini propaganda in Padua

In a book describing an imaginary trial of Mussolini in 1945 the words of an Italian give an interesting view on how blame can be allocated for the rise of Fascism: "It was Italians who first fought Fascism in Europe. They fought Fascism when many others who now lay the guilt on the whole bulk of the Italian people were fawning on it . . . When I hear some persons of other nationalities who assisted Mussolini in reducing the Italian people to servitude now condemning the whole nation for their subservience to Fascism I am reminded of an answer once given by the Emperor Julian. 'An orphan!' he cried. 'Does the murderer of my father upbraid me that I am orphan?' (176)."

Eventually Fascism became less of an ideology that was tied to a party and more of a way of life to be accepted. This point is illustrated by a story invented by the Italians: "The Secretary of the Fascist Party visits a large factory, accompanied by the company director. At the end of the tour all the workers are massed in the yard to listen to a speech. Before addressing them the Fascist chief asks the director: 'What are these people's politics?' The director answers: 'One-third of them are Communist, one-third Socialist, and the rest belong to several small parties.' The Fascist's face turns livid. 'What?' he cries, 'And how many of them are Fascist?' The director reassures him quickly: 'All of them, Your Excellency, all of them.' (177)"

Playing safe Italians, except for Mussolini's most fanatical supporters learned to "play safe", to give superficial loyalty to Fascism while waiting for better times. No one knew when seeming advantage would become a disastrous liability overnight.

A journalist, Luigi Barzini, recounts one personal experience: "In April, 1940, a commissioner of police arrested me for being a dangerous enemy of the Fascist regime, he was inordinately polite. While I waited at the *Questura* [court] to be interrogated, he sent for a good dinner from the nearest trattoria, sent to my house for clean shirts, a change of clothes and some money, and warned me veiledly about what was best to say and not to say when questioned . . . I thanked him and asked him why he had been so kind. He frankly said: 'One never knows. Maybe you'll be able to do the same for me, some day.' The regime was

A map showing territory acquired by Italy between 1939 and 1943

still very powerful and unchallenged at the time . . . The commissioner was carefully buying insurance against a most improbable event (178)."

Carlo Levi, a writer and doctor, was banished by Mussolini in 1935 to the isolated village of Gagliano in the South. Here he records the attitude of the peasants towards Fascism: "They have no conception of political struggle; they think of it as a personal quarrel among the 'fellows in Rome'. They are not concerned with the views of the political prisoners who were in compulsory residence among them, or with the motives for their coming. They looked at them kindly and treated them like brothers because they too, for some inexplicable reasons, were victims of fate (179)."

Of the desolate area of Lucania, in the mountainous central

The "other" Italy

97

region of southernmost Italy Levi remarked: "Christ never came this far, nor did time, nor the individual soul, nor hope, nor the relation of cause to effect, nor reason nor history. No-one has come to this land except as an enemy, a conqueror, or a visitor devoid of understanding. The seasons pass to-day over the toil of the peasants, just as they did three thousand years before Christ; no message, human or divine, has reached this stubborn poverty (180)."

Mussolini's appeal

Why did Mussolini have such a popular appeal for the people? Max Ascoli, editor of Mussolini's book *Fall of Mussolini*, wrote that "He always knew how to speak a language that the people understood . . . He had all sorts of feelers and antennae that made him grasp the trend of popular mood and suggested to him the right attitude, the right slogan, that could bring popular passion to a frenzy (181)." Typical of his phrases, punctuated by lengthy pauses and calculated to disarm any hostile crowd, were "Sons of Julius Caesar . . . Sons of Michael Angelo . . . I come to you as a brother."

Mussolini said of himself: "I have annihilated in myself every egotism: I, like the most devoted of citizens, place upon myself and on every beat of my heart service to the Italian people (182)."

Mussolini's Fascist biographer, Giorgio Pini, described the personalized nature of Fascism: "It is getting to be more and more difficult to distinguish the private from the public aspects of Mussolini's life. His biography has come to be the history of the Italian nation. In the leading principles of government the figure of the head of the Government cannot be separated from his human personality; the phrase which a working man addressed to him while he was threshing wheat in the reclaimed Pontine area, 'You are all of us, rather than an intuition, was a statement of fact expressed in simple language.' (183)"

Mussolini the actor

Ugo Ojetti, an art critic and admirer of Mussolini wrote, "I cannot help thinking when I see him, how much his face must ache at night when he retires (184)." Like a born actor he had a way of enthralling the crowds that saw and listened to him. "That he was conscious of playing roles all the time could be discerned by any attentive observer: he walked, strutted or

Opposite Mussolini, in a dramatic pose, speaking in Rome

strode like a tragedian wearing an ancient costume; he pivoted on one spurred boot heel as if he were always trailing a long purple cloak behind him. He never tired but never looked at ease (185)."

Laura Fermi's comment was: "Benito Mussolini's vitality was in itself an element of attraction, a cause for admiration; but it was not the main factor. Most of those who came under his spell said that his charm was something that defied definition (186)." These observations were confirmed by Pini: "When receiving visitors he at once puts them at their ease and they experience no timidity before the man whom they had long wished to meet, even though they might feel some awe at the idea of meeting him; he is perfectly simple in manner and knows how to place himself on the psychological plane of his visitor. His personality undoubtedly fascinates even the most bitter opponents (187)."

The Japanese Ambassador, Yosuke Matsuoka, said, "I am convinced that it is not only the art of government which makes of him an incomparable man. His speeches are inspired by a human force which raises him above all the ideas of all peoples; he is yours, but he belongs to the world (188)."

His colourful actor-like expressions adorned many posters. In a country where a large section of the people were illiterate they made an effective appeal. One contemporary wrote: "Many of Mussolini's educational ideas find expression in phrases, inscriptions, and slogans engraved, sculpted, or stencilled on monuments and public and private buildings all over the country, such as Book and rifle, To live dangerously, Rome dominates, We shall drive ahead, To go towards the people, Many foes, much honour, He who stops still is lost . . . (189)"

One on occasion Mussolini stirred the popular imagination with the comment: "If I go forward follow me; if I yield, kill me; if I die, avenge me (190)."

5 Foreign Ventures and Mussolini's Downfall

MUSSOLINI HAD boundless ambition. He wanted to revive ancient Roman glories of Empire, which Italy before 1914 had little success in achieving. In 1921 he declared: "It is destined that the Mediterranean should become ours, that Rome should be the directing city of civilization in the whole of the West of Europe (191)."

Italy's foreign policy in the 1920s was comparatively peaceful. By 1928, with Fascism firmly installed at home Mussolini declared: "Fascism, as regards ideas, doctrine, realization, is universal. One can foresee a Fascist Europe, a Europe which draws inspiration for its institutions from the doctrines and practices of Fascism ... (192)" Soon he was calling for re-armament and the revision of European treaties.

Fascism—a universal idea

Full of restless energy, he never seemed to tire of talking about the value of war. In 1934 he said: "To begin with, history tells us that war is the phenomenon which accompanies the development of man ... War is for man what motherhood is for woman ... not only do I not believe in everlasting peace, but I would also hold it as depressing and destructive of the basic virtues of man, which only in a bloody effort can shine in the full light of the sun (193)."

On numerous occasions Mussolini urged the Italians to be warlike: "The legend that the Italians are not fighters must be dispelled; for yesterday, as today, the prestige of nations is determined almost absolutely by their military glories and their armed power (194)." The Ten Commandments of the Fascist fighter included (195):

The Fascist fighter

101

"(1) Know that the Fascist and particularly the soldier must not believe in perpetual peace.

"(8) Mussolini is always right.

"(10) One thing must be dear to you above all; the life of the Duce."

Many people had considerable doubts about Fascism. The system was lightened by numerous anti-Fascist jokes which also partly reflected the current attitudes to Mussolini: "The Duce is proud of his legions. The story goes that when Mr. Anthony Eden called on him in June, 1935, he said: 'Look at these electric buttons on my desk. With them I can get into touch with all my Ministries . . . yellow for the colonies, green for foreign affairs, and this red one . . . Ah, I have only to press it and a million men will be mobilized at once.' The Lord Privy Seal looked hard at the red button. 'What would happen if you pressed it by mistake when you wanted a sandwich and a glass of beer?' he asked blandly. Rome laughed heartily over this invention, which is said to have originated from the Italian War Ministry (196)."

Causes of the Abyssinian War (1935) Mussolini was driven to his first foreign venture as a need to divert people's attention from home affairs. Giuseppe Borgese, one of the University professors who had refused to take the Fascist loyalty oath in 1931, wrote of Mussolini, "Dissatisfaction and sarcasm were rankling in the impoverished country . . . He [Mussolini] himself admitted that the bottom of economic depression had been reached, and that there was no way further down. War, the initial purpose of his career, had now also become the only way out (197)." It was hoped the conflict would revive the regime's popularity and that Abyssinia might provide an outlet for over-population.

In 1935 Mussolini seized upon a border incident at Wal Wal as the excuse. Abyssinia lay between the Italian colonies of Eritrea and Somaliland. The war was justified by Marshal Pietro Badoglio: "to rid ourselves of a perpetual threat to our Eastern African colonies and to remedy the insufferable wrongs committed by a barbarous state against our thousand year-old civilizations (198)."

"Better to live for one day as a lion than a thousand years

Italian soldiers attacking the Northern front in the Abyssinian War

as a lamb," encouraged the Duce as his men left for the war. *Embarkation* A correspondent of the London newspaper, *The Times*, describes *of troops* the embarkation of troops in Naples: "Now and again a voice rising above the other cries 'Greet the Duce', and thousands of voices answer 'To us'. Then all repeat in chorus 'Du–ce', 'Du–ce', 'Du–ce', stressing strongly the 'ce'. Now and again voices rise above the others 'To whom Abyssinia' and the soldiers' reply comes in chorus 'To us' or 'To whom the glory?' and the soldiers again: 'To us'. Bands on the quay play the Fascist revolutionary anthems. The soldiers sing old and new war songs (199)."

And so half a million soldiers descended upon Abyssinia. The label "barbarous" may, more appropriately, have been applied to the Italian forces, against which the poorly armed native troops could only offer token resistance. The Militia car-

103

ried an image of fighting glory: "At the first crackle of musketry the Black Shirts will see again the powerful figure of the Duce. They will see it thrown against the background of the sky beyond the enemy like a gigantic vision of a warlike dream. At that vision the Black Shirts, terrible and splendid will smash every resistance, bombs in their hands, daggers between their teeth and a sovereign contempt for danger in their hearts (200)."

Mussolini's son, Vittorio Mussolini, took a sadistic glee in the war in his book *Flying over Ethiopian Mountain Ranges*. He found the war a period of "magnificent sport . . . one group of horsemen gave me the impression of a budding rose unfolding as the bombs fell in their midst, and blew them up. It was exceptionally good fun (201)." In the Abyssinian war, Italy was the first country to use poison gas.

Sanctions

What did the rest of Europe think of Italy's actions? The League of Nations branded Italy as the aggressor and ordered sanctions against her. However, these sanctions did not include coal and oil and proved to be quite ineffective. They did not hold up the war effort in the least.

Also, the Soviet Union, Germany and the United States were not bound by the embargo and continued to trade with Italy. By May, 1936, the war was over. Haile Selassie lived as a refugee in Britain, and King Victor Emmanuel of Italy became Emperor of Abyssinia.

Revival of popularity

After Italy's victory in Abyssinia Mussolini was idolized more than ever. "His pictures were cut out of newspapers and magazines and pasted on the walls of poor peasant cottages, at the side of the Madonna and Saint Joseph. School girls fell in love with him as a film star. His more memorable words were written large on village houses for all to read. One of his collaborators exclaimed, after listening to him announce from the balcony that Abyssinia had been conquered and that Rome had again become the Capital of an Empire . . . 'He is like a god . . .' 'Like a god? No, no' said another, 'He is a god.' (202)"

Gabriele D'Annunzio in a message to Mussolini said: "After so many battles, so many conflicts, so much will-power, you have indeed achieved that which in the history of great men is hardly ever achieved—you have created your own legend (203)."

104

Opposite The King of Italy and Mussolini with General Montanari and General Petitti di Roveto

The Spanish *Civil War* *(1936–39)* With the start of the Civil War in Spain in 1936 Mussolini saw a chance for Fascism to take over the southern Mediterranean. He sent over 70,000 soldiers to fight on the side of General Franco and the Army, who were in revolt against the Republic. Because Franco had the support of the Church, the nobility and all the right-wing elements—the chief being the Fascist Falangist party, Mussolini felt sure of a quick victory. But he had not reckoned on the Republican resistance which extended the hostilities until 1939. Though Franco eventually won, Mussolini's dreams were thwarted since his aid in men and supplies of raw material had been a heavy drain on Italian finances.

Galeazzo Ciano, the Italian Foreign Minister, recorded his impressions at a presentation of medals to the widows of men killed in Spain: "As I watched these men and women in mourning file by . . . I examined my conscience and asked myself whether this blood had been shed in a good cause. Yes, the answer is yes. At Malaga, at Guadalajara, at Santander, we were fighting in defence of our civilization and our revolution (204)."

The Rome- *Berlin Axis* *(1936)* In 1936 Mussolini signed the Rome-Berlin Axis agreement of friendship with Germany. He felt this alliance with Germany, another dictatorship, secured his position in Europe while Italy pursued policies in the Mediterranean and in Africa. But it was to prove his undoing. Mussolini fell under Hitler's spell, and was later to form a military alliance with Germany. He also introduced anti-Semitism in Italy. These two acts were bitterly resented by the Italians. He miscalculated in believing Germany would win any future war and that it would pay him to be on her side.

The "goose *step"* In admiration of the slick militarism of the Germans Mussolini introduced the "goose step" into the Italian forces. He refused to admit that he had imitated the Germans by arguing that the goose was a Roman animal which had once saved the Capitol from the Gauls!

Count Dino Grandi, diplomat and respected member of the Fascist hierarchy, wrote enthusiastically about the step to Mussolini: "The ground trembled under the thud, or rather the hammering of the legionnaires' feet. I looked from close by at our Black Shirts. When they march in 'Roman Step' their eyes sparkle, the line of their mouths is hard and narrow and there is a new expression on their faces, which is not just conventionally martial, but reflects the pride of a warrior who splits and crushes the enemy's head beneath his heel (205)."

Despite all his warlike postures and speeches Mussolini had no wish for a war. When war seemed imminent in 1938, due to Hitler's threats to Czechoslovakia, he introduced a peace conference at the request of the British Prime Minister, Neville Chamberlain. On 29th September, war was averted by the signing of the Munich Agreement—but not for long. In March, 1939, Hitler, who was dissatisfied with the Munich Agreement, extended his rule over the whole of Czechoslovakia. And Mussolini, who was unable to resist the appeal to power, invaded Albania. *Munich Agreement (1938)*

It was then that Mussolini took the fatal step of pledging full military support for Germany in the Pact of Steel. This military alliance was unique in that it was the first which, quite openly, offered support for a war of aggression. Article III of the Pact stated: "If in spite of the desires and hopes of the contracting powers, it should happen that one of them should become involved in warlike complications with one or more foreign powers, the other contracting power agrees as an ally to come immediately to its side and to sustain it with all of its military forces, on land, the seas and in the air (206)." *Pact of Steel (1939)*

On 1st September, 1939, Hitler invaded Poland. Mussolini told Hitler that Italy was not ready for war, and Hitler released him from his promise. Mussolini soon felt that this was a sign of weakness, which made him the laughing stock of Europe. So on 10th June, 1940, when German victory seemed assured against France Mussolini declared war on France and Britain, without consulting the Fascist Council or the people. He hoped to pick up without effort some spoils from a quick war. *Beginning of Second World War (1939–43)*

However, Italy was drawn into a long conflict which completely upset Mussolini's plans. His advisors had made it clear that Italian industry would not be in a position to provide the means for total war until late 1943 at the earliest. On 11th August, 1939, Count Ciano, the Italian Foreign Minister and *Italy's unpreparedness*

107

Overleaf Italian soldiers fighting for Franco in the Spanish Civil War

Two dictators: Mussolini and Hitler in Munich

Mussolini's son-in-law, had given Joachim von Ribbentrop, the German Foreign Minister, a similar warning: "It was impossible materially, and politically, militarily and psychologically for Italy to participate in a war at this early state. She had, in effect, been waging war for years on end. What with intervention in the Spanish Civil War and the conquest of the Abyssinian Empire, the Italian people had been pushed into one armed conflict after another, and the result was a pronounced degree of war weariness. In addition these years had virtually exhausted Italy's scant stock of materials (207)."

Marshal Badoglio, the Army General Staff exclaimed to Mussolini: "Do you not know that we have not enough shirts for our soldiers—I do not say uniforms, but shirts." The Duce's blunt reply was: "I know, but I need only a few thousand dead, so that I shall be able to sit at the peace table with the victor (208)."

Public reaction   As far as the people of Italy were concerned, Eugene Dollman, the German interpreter in Rome, wrote: "Though disunited as only 50,000,000 individualists can be," the ordinary people

German troops in Warsaw, Poland, at the beginning of the war

"were virtually unanimous in their willingness to do anything rather than fight a war on Germany's side (209)."

An Italian described the reaction of the people: "Three aspects of the war aroused special bewilderment and distress: that the war should be against Poland, with whom Italy, from the earliest Risorgimento times, has had special links and sympathy; against Belgium, the 'brave little country' of the last war . . . and above all, against England. Also, an old rhyme came back into circulation: 'With any country war, but never England'. As for war with America, that remained almost beyond credibility (210)."

By the time of the French surrender on 24th June, Italian forces had made little headway against the French. Consequently Mussolini secured nothing from the armistice arrangements to Italy's benefit.

Italian defeats

Determined to restore his prestige the Duce attacked Egypt. From now on till the final defeat of the Germans in Italy in May, 1945, the Italians suffered one humiliation after another. She was pushed back in Greece, which was taken by the Germans who then occupied most of the vital positions in Italy. In 1941 Abyssinia was lost, and in 1942 Italian contingents who had been sent to the Russian front suffered heavy losses. In North Africa the German, General Rommel, took over, but by 1943 he was completely defeated.

Why did the Italian forces suffer such devastation? Two wounded soldiers discussing the situation, in the front at the Battle of El Alamein (1942), blamed it on poor leadership.

111

Count Sillavengo recounts the conversation in his war memoirs:
"'The big mistake,' said a Sicilian voice, 'was to let the war
be run by a Bersaglieri corporal dressed up as a Field-Marshal
and surrounded by a staff of yes men!' 'And what would you
have done then?' demanded a Milanese." The reply was to get
any businessman from Milan called Mr. Ambrogio Brambilla
to run the war. He was then told that there were ten pages of
Brambillas in the telephone directory, at least two columns of
Ambrogio's, half of whom at least would be business men.
"'Pick one at random,' said the Sicilian with an air of finality
'Any single one of 'em would be better than the bloke who's
running things at the moment!' (211)"

The troops themselves were in a sorry state. Ciano mentions
one incident in his diary: "I have given the Duce a serious and
harsh letter from Professor Faccini of Leghorn, whose eighteen
year-old son, mobilized on 17th January, was sent to Albania
on the same day, without knowing what a firearm was. This
explains so many things (212)."

Ill-equipped and ill-prepared to face war, the soldiers
placed the blame on Mussolini: "Hungry and tired the
Italian troops march into Nice. The population, including many
Italians, is silent. Suddenly one civilian shouts 'Long live the
Duce!' An Officer turns to the unwanted enthusiast and says
'You go back to Italy, then you will see whether you will dare
to shout that' (213)."

German-Italian relations Mussolini, in turn, blamed Germany for failing to supply the
necessary promised materials. Bitterly he exclaimed: "Among
the cemeteries I shall some day build the most important of all,
one in which to bury German promises. They have delivered
nothing, or almost nothing, of what they promised." Perhaps
his anger was raised by a joke circulating in Germany: "In two
months we shall win the war against Russia, in four months
against Great Britain, and in four days against Italy (214)."

The Resistance From 1941 resistance against Mussolini, and the war grew.
Groups of Italian and Yugoslavian anti-Fascists worked together
to publish several underground newspapers which succeeded in
persuading soldiers to desert the Fascist army. The racist elements
of Nazism and Fascism brought thousands of Italians into a

112

Resistance movement. In 1942 the Italian High Command in its French sector requested the Vichy Government to:

"(1) Revoke immediately all arrests of Jews.

"(2) To order at once all prefects of Italian occupied France to refrain from any act or discrimination against Jews, to whatever nationality they belong.

"(3) To release without delay all those who had been arrested (215)."

In 1943 a document sent by the anti-Fascists to Britain outlined the aims of the Resistance in Italy: "'The present goal of the free patriotic Italians, grouped together in Italy in the Committee of Action for the Union of the Italian people (C.U.P.I.) is the preparation and immediate organization of the national insurrection for national liberation, to get rid of Mussolini's traitor government, drive out the Germans, sign an immediate peace with the United Nations and range our country beside the United Nations in the fight for the liberation of Italy and all the peoples under the yoke of Hitlerism and Fascism.' It described itself as 'an organization which, although springing originally from the initiative of the traditional anti-Fascists, united Italians of all political trends from opposition Fascists to Catholics, Monarchists, Liberals, Socialists and Communists.' (216)"

With hatred of Mussolini increasing in all sectors of the country, the final rejection came, ironically, from his own men. *Mussolini's downfall* Ciano and a group of Fascists, realizing the war was lost, now regarded Mussolini as a burden. Pressure was put upon the King by Marshal Badoglio, and the Chief of Staff, General Ambrosia, to force the Duce's resignation. They ensured that General Raffaele Cadorna would be ready to force a change of government if the King failed to oust Mussolini. The event was hastened by the Allied landing in Sicily on 10th July, which was welcomed by most of the local people, and met with little resistance from the army.

On 24th July the Grand Council voted nineteen to four in favour of Count Dino Grandi's motion calling for all national institutions to resume their original functions and the King to assume supreme command of the armed forces. Grandi told

113

Mussolini: "You believe you have the devotion of the people
.... You lost it the day you tied Italy to Germany (217)."

*Audience with
the King* Despite the people's lack of confidence in his leadership,
Mussolini had so lost touch with reality that he had little idea
of what was in store for him. He described his next experience:
"I entered the Villa Ada, therefore with a mind completely free
from any forebodings, in a state, which looking back on it,
might really be called utterly unsuspecting (218)." The king
ushered him into the drawing room. Distraught and speaking
indistinctly, he said: "My dear Duce, it can't go on any longer.
Italy is in pieces. Army morale has reached the bottom . . . the
Alpine regiments have a song saying that they are through
fighting Mussolini's war. Surely you have no illusions as to how
Italians feel about you at this moment. You are the most hated
man in Italy; you have not a single friend left except for me
(219)."

This was certainly near the truth. In any case his soldiers did
not want him; some of them in an underground newspaper
appeal published: "Who are we? What do we want? We are
soldiers of Italy, which we want to liberate from Mussolini. We
shall not fight for the Germans, no. We are not at the service of
the oppressors, but rather we serve freedom. We want immediately to use our weapons to help the people of France
regain its independence . . . (220)"

*Badoglio's
government* Stunned by his dismissal, Mussolini allowed himself to be
placed under "protective custody". He was told this was for his
own safety, but in reality he was under arrest. Marshal Badoglio
became head of the government and all Fascist institutions were
gradually dismantled. On 3rd September Badoglio signed an
armistice with the Allies. Hitler, who had anticipated this, had
already sent German troops in force into Italy. On 8th September,
the King and Badoglio, fearing a German occupation of Rome,
fled to the South.

*The Salo
Republic* On Hitler's orders, Mussolini was recaptured by German
glider troops on 12th September. Though now a sick man,
Mussolini agreed to create a new Italian state in the North to
keep as many Italians as possible loyal to the Axis. He had no
real power and was completely under the control of the German

Opposite King Victor Emmanuel with Mussolini

authorities. Eventually some of those who had voted against him in the Grand Council meeting of 25th July were caught and sentenced to death. These included Ciano and de Bono.

Civil war In Italy for the next twenty months there was not only war by foreign powers but also civil war between Italians. In the South the King's government were the puppets of the Allies. Many Italians in the North joined the Resistance to harry the German forces and the Italian Fascists who were loyal to Mussolini.

Italian forces now joined the Allies against Germany and fought more vigorously than they had ever done under Fascism. Some Italian units, though hopelessly outnumbered, preferred to fight rather than surrender to the Germans. Typical of situations facing Italian prisoners-of-war were the choices offered to them at one centre in France. These were: "(1) Returning to fight Britain. (2) Work in Germany as freed prisoners. (3) Concentration Camp. Result: 1st Solution—0, 2nd—67, 3rd—336. And this although the soldiers know what it meant to be in a German Concentration Camp considered and treated as traitors (221)."

Italians in the North had to decide whether to continue to live peaceably under Fascism or to join the Resistance. A surprising number chose the latter course.

Natalia Ginzburg, an anti-Fascist, describes the experiences of one family. They wondered whether to "call a meeting of the locals and arrange to hide behind hedges and shoot at the Germans at night, or at least to scatter nails along the road. Cenzo Rena, one of the group, because they had met a German who was a waiter and had got to know him well, said he would not shoot straight if given a pistol or a tommy-gun. He would have started thinking things which it was not right to think, that the Germans were all waiters, poor unfortunates with some sort of job at the back of them, poor unfortunates whom it was not really worthwhile killing. And this was a thought that in war-time had no sense, it was an idiotic thought but he himself might happen to have an idiotic thought of that kind (222)." Later he did kill the German in self-defence.

116 When, in retaliation, Italian hostages were taken by the

Germans, Cenzo Rena went to see the commandant to get their release. He was shot. After this more hostages were taken by the Germans, a girl, two men and a shepherd boy of fourteen. They were put in the mayor's stable which was then burnt down. Typical of the Italian people's acceptance of these terrible acts of brutality was this reaction: "No-one could understand why the Germans should have burnt down the stable with the cows and the people inside, but perhaps it was only because they had some petrol to throw away (223)." *German reprisals*

In Turin in January, 1944, the Germans backed up reprisals against partisan attacks with the following regulations:

"(1) Anyone possessing weapons or hiding partisans (members of the Resistance) will immediately be shot;

"(2) German soldiers will use their weapons against any gathering of more than two persons;

"(3) Villages whose inhabitants insult German soldiers will be razed to the ground (224)."

The Italians retaliated by calling a general strike: "The factory sirens will blow at ten o'clock on the morning of 1st March . . . when you hear them, walk out. You will remain on strike until we tell you to go back. But you must stay out whatever happens (225)." The results were that "scores of Italian workmen were shot down, minor pitched battles were fought in the streets of Italian cities at night, every possible pressure was put on the strikers, but the ranks were never broken once (226)." The strike quickly spread to the other major towns in the North, causing disruption in the German war effort. *A general strike*

By April, 1945, German resistance to the Allies in Italy was over. Mussolini fled to the mountains outside Milan, and joined a convoy of retreating Germans. It was not long, however, before Resistance men stopped the convoy and found Mussolini, disguised in a German greatcoat and army boots, huddled in the corner of a lorry. He was shot on the order of the Committee of National Liberation for Upper Italy, and his body was strung upside down with that of his mistress in Milan. *Death of Mussolini*

Thus died the man of whom Luigi Barzini wrote, "had played a versatile multifaced role, that of Mussolini, a heroic mixture of the Renaissance *condottiere*, cold Machiavellian thinker, *Final verdict*

Lenin-like leader of a revolutionary minority, steely minded dictator, humanitarian despot, Casanova lover and Nietzschean superman. He added later to his repertoire the Napoleonic genius, with well-known results, and, just before he died, the socialist renovator of society. He was none of these things. In the end, like an old actor, he no longer remembered what he really was, felt, believed and wanted (227)."

Barzini concluded: "The explanation of his failure is perhaps that he was not a failure. He lost the war, power, his country, his mistress, his place in history and his life, but succeeded in what he had wanted to do since he took power . . . he had dedicated his life just to putting up a good show, a stirring show (228)."

But when the show had disintegrated and the end was near in 1944 Mussolini admitted with regret: "When I allied myself with Hitler I took a leap in the dark; but after all the Germans were Fascists.' He stopped exhausted then added in a broken tone, 'I forgot that as a statesman I had the fate of millions of people in my hands.' (229)"

The mutilated bodies of Mussolini and his mistress having been shot by Resistance men

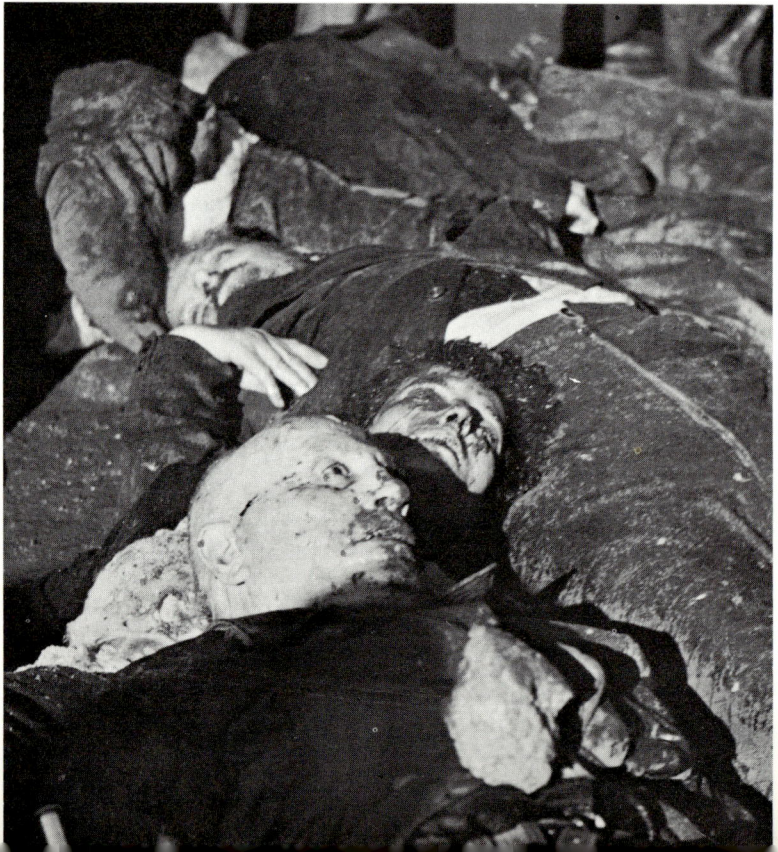

Table of Events

1914

November — Mussolini expelled from *Avanti* and the Socialist Party

15th November — Mussolini starts his own newspaper *Il Popolo d'Italia*

1919

23rd March — Fasci di Combattimento (*Battle Squads*) formed at Milan

12th September — D'Annunzio captures Fiume

November — General Election (universal male suffrage). Large gains for Socialists and Popular Party (*Popolari*)

1920

September — Occupation of factories by workers in Northern Italy

1921

January — Split of members at Socialist Congress. The Italian Communist Party founded

May — General Election. Mussolini and thirty-four other Fascists elected to Parliament

7th–10th November — National Fascist Party (P.N.F.) formed from the Fascist movement

1922

January — Corporations formed by Michele Bianchi within the Fascist Party

20th September — Mussolini speaks in favour of the Monarchy

24th–26th October — Fascist Party Congress held at Naples

28th October — March on Rome

30th October — Mussolini becomes Prime Minister

December — Creation of Fascist Grand Council

1923

14th January — Squads transformed into Fascist Militia

February — Nationalist Party merges with the Fascists

| April | Resignation of members of Popular Party from Mussolini's Coalition government |
| November | Acerbo Law |

1924

6th April	General Election
10th June	Murder of Matteotti
13th June	Aventine Secession led by Giovanni Amendola

1925

3rd January	Mussolini assumes full responsibility for past activities of Fascist Party. Beginning of Dictatorial rule
1st May	Dopolavoro created
2nd October	The Palazzo Vidoni Pact
24th December	Ministers made responsible to Mussolini rather than to the King

1926

3rd April	Balilla youth organization created Adoption of the Fascist calendar
28th October	Zaniboni's attempt on Mussolini's life
25th November	Formation of Special Tribunal

1927

| 21st April | The Labour Charter |
| September | Savona trial of Rosselli and Pari |

1928

| January | Gramsci sentenced to twenty year's imprisonment |
| 17th May | New electoral law abolishes normal voting procedures |

1929

11th February	Lateran Agreements
24th March	Plebiscitary-type election
December	Formation of National Council of Corporations

1931

| 29th June | Papal Encyclical *Non abbiamo bisogno* |

1935

| 3rd October | Abyssinia attacked by Italy |

1936

9th May	Victor Emmanuel III becomes Emperor of Abyssinia
July	Start of Spanish Civil War
1st November	Formation of Rome-Berlin Axis

1938

29th September	Munich Conference over Czechoslovakia
17th November	Introduction of Anti-Semitic legislation

1939

19th January	Chamber of Deputies replaced by Assembly of Corporations
22nd May	Pact of Steel
3rd September	Start of Second World War

1940

10th June	Mussolini declares war on Britain and France
28th October	Mussolini attacks Greece

1943

March	Massive strikes in Turin and Milan
10th July	Landing of Allied forces in Sicily
24th–25th July	Grand Council meeting. Lack of Confidence expressed in Mussolini's rule
26th July	Mussolini dismissed from office by the King
3rd September	Italy signs an Armistice with the Allies
12th September	German troops rescue Mussolini from hands of Marshal Badoglio's government
September	Committee of National Liberation formed from the Resistance Movement

1944

11th January	Execution of Ciano after Verona trial in Mussolini's Salo Republic
4th June	Allies liberate Rome

1945

28th April	Execution of Mussolini

Notes on Sources

(1) Fermi, Mussolini (Chicago, 1961)
(2) *Ibid*
(3) Lussu, *Enter Mussolini* (London, 1936) Trans. Marion Rawson
(4) Fermi, *op. cit.*
(5) Lussu, *op. cit.*
(6) Delzell, Ed. *Mediterranean Fascism 1919–1945*—selected documents (London, 1971)
(7) Kemechey, *Il Duce* (New York, 1930)
(8) *Ibid*
(9) *Ibid*
(10) Nenni, *Ten Years of Tyranny in Italy* (London, 1932) Trans. Anne Steele
(11) *Ibid*
(12) Lussu, *op. cit.*
(13) *Ibid*
(14) *Ibid*
(15) Fermi, *op. cit.*
(16) Lussu, *op. cit.*
(17) Fermi, *op. cit.*
(18) Delzell, *op. cit.*
(19) Rossi (Tasca), *The Rise of Italian Fascism 1918–22* (London, 1938)
(20) *Ibid*
(21) Sturzo, *Italy and Fascism* (London, 1926)
(22) Mussolini, *My Autobiography* (London, 1931) Trans. R. W. Child
(23) *Ibid*
(24) Lussu, *op. cit.*
(25) Nenni, *op. cit.*
(26) *Ibid*
(27) Quoted in Dollman, *The Interpreter* (London, 1967) Trans. J.

Maxwell Brownjohn
(28) Nenni, *op. cit.*
(29) Mussolini, *op. cit.*
(30) Barzini, *The Italians* (London, 1964)
(31) Delzell, *op. cit.*
(32) Salvemini, *The Fascist Dictatorship in Italy* (New York, 1927)
(33) Lussu, *op. cit.*
(34) Salvemini, *op. cit.*
(35) Lussu, *op. cit.*
(36) Salvemini, *op. cit.*
(37) *Ibid*
(38) *Ibid*
(39) Monelli, *Mussolini* (London, 1953)
(40) *Ibid*
(41) Salvemini, *op. cit.*
(42) Matteotti, *The Fascisti Exposed* (London, 1924) Trans. E. W. Dickes
(43) Nenni, *op. cit.*
(44) *Ibid*
(45) Smith, *Italy* (Ann Arbor, 1959)
(46) Rosengarten, *The Italian Anti-Fascist Press 1919–45* (Cleveland, 1966)
(47) Delzell, *op. cit.*
(48) Quoted in Smith, *op. cit.*
(49) Fermi, *op. cit.*
(50) Delzell, *op. cit.*
(51) *Ibid*
(52) Rappard, *Source Book on European Government* (New York, 1937)
(53) Delzell, *op. cit.*
(54) Nenni, *op. cit.*
(55) Delzell, *op. cit.*
(56) *Ibid*
(57) Salvemini, *Under the*

Axe of Fascism (New York, 1936)
(58) Hamilton, *Modern Italy* (London, 1932)
(59) Rappard, *op. cit.*
(60) Ludwig, *Talks with Mussolini* (London, 1932) Trans. Eden & Cedar Paul
(61) *Ibid*
(62) Fermi, *op. cit.*
(63) *Ibid*
(64) Seldes, *Sawdust Caesar* (New York, 1935)
(65) Kemechey, *op. cit.*
(66) *Ibid*
(67) Delzell, *op. cit.*
(68) *Ibid*
(69) *Ibid*
(70) *The Spectator*, February 6, 1932, quoted in Salvemini, *Under the Axe of Fascism, op. cit.*
(71) Partito Nazionale Fascisto (Rome, 1937)
(72) Seldes, *op. cit.*
(73) Hamilton, *op. cit.*
(74) Balbo, *My Air Armada* (London, 1934) Trans. Gerald Griffin
(75) *Ibid*
(76) Seldes, *op. cit.*
(77) Finer, *Mussolini's Italy* (London, 1935)
(78) Seldes, *op. cit.*
(79) *Ibid*
(80) *Ibid*
(81) *Ibid*
(82) Monelli, *op. cit.*
(83) *Ibid*
(84) Pini, *The Official Life of Mussolini* (London, 1939)
(85) *Ibid*
(86) Finer, *op. cit.*

(87) Hamilton, *op. cit.*
(88) Seldes, *op. cit.*
(89) Hamilton, *op. cit.*
(90) Finer, *op. cit.*
(91) Smith, *op. cit.*
(92) Hamilton, *op. cit.*
(93) *Ibid*
(94) Delzell, *op. cit.*
(95) *Ibid*
(96) *Ibid*
(97) Finer, *op. cit.*
(98) Hamilton, *op. cit.*
(99) Finer, *op. cit.*
(100) *Ibid*
(101) *Ibid*
(102) *Ibid*
(103) Binchy, *Church and State in Fascist Italy* (London, 1964)
(104) *Ibid*
(105) *Ibid*
(106) Delzell, *op. cit.*
(107) *Ibid*
(108) *Ibid*
(109) *Ibid*
(110) Binchy, *op. cit.*
(111) *Ibid*
(112) *Ibid*
(113) The Ciano Diaries (1937–8) Ed. Andreas Mayer
(114) Delzell, *op. cit.*
(115) Binchy, *op. cit.*
(116) Clough & Saladino, *A History of Modern Italy —Documents, Readings and Commentary* (New York, 1968)
(117) Ginzburg, *Dead Yesterdays* (London, 1956) Trans. A. Davidson
(118) Hibbert, *Benito Mussolini* (London, 1963)
(119) Sforza, *Contemporary Italy* (London, 1946)
(120) *Ibid*
(121) Finer, *op. cit.*
(122) *Ibid*
(123) Salvemini, *The Fascist Dictatorship in Italy*, *op. cit.*
(124) *Ibid*
(125) *Ibid*
(126) *Ibid*
(127) Reut-Nicolussi, *Tyrol under the Axe of Fascism* (London, 1930) Trans. K. L. Montgomery
(128) *The Times* (8th November, 1926)
(129) Lussu, *op. cit.*
(130) Nitti, *Escape* (1930)
(131) Delzell, *op. cit.*
(132) *Ibid*
(133) Tiltman, *The Terror in Europe* (London, 1931)
(134) *Ibid*
(135) Seldes, *op. cit.*
(136) Lussu, *op. cit.*
(137) *Ibid*
(138) Tiltman, *op. cit.*
(139) Nitti, *op. cit.*
(140) Lussu, *op. cit.*
(141) Nitti, *op. cit.*
(142) Salvemini, *The Fascist Dictatorship in Italy*, *op. cit.*
(143) *Ibid*
(144) *Ibid*
(145) *Ibid*
(146) *Ibid*
(147) Tiltman, *op. cit.*
(148) Salvemini, *The Fascist Dictatorship in Italy*, *op. cit.*
(149) Rosengarten, *op. cit.*
(150) Nitti, *op. cit.*
(151) Rosengarten, *op. cit.*
(152) *Ibid*
(153) Nitti, *op. cit.*
(154) Rosengarten, *op. cit.*
(155) Tiltman, *op. cit.*
(156) Delzell, *op. cit.*
(157) Lussu Salvadori, *Freedom has no Frontier* (London, 1969)
(158) *Ibid*
(159) Tiltman, *op. cit.*
(160) *Ibid*
(161) Salvadori, *op. cit.*
(162) Hughes, *The Fall and Rise of Modern Italy* (New York, 1967)
(163) Delzell, *Mussolini's Enemies* (Princeton, 1961)
(164) De Bosis, *The Story of my Death* (New York, 1933)
(165) Quoted in Sforza, *op. cit.*
(166) Lewis, *The Honoured Society* (London, 1964)
(167) *Ibid*
(168) Nitti, *op. cit.*
(169) *Ibid*
(170) Reut-Nicolussi, *op. cit.*
(171) *Ibid*
(172) *Ibid*
(173) *Ibid*
(174) *Ibid*
(175) King, *Fascism in Italy* (London, 1931)
(176) "Cassius", *The Trial of Mussolini* (London, 1943)
(177) Barzini, *op. cit.*
(178) *Ibid*
(179) Levi, *Christ Stopped at Eboli* (New York, 1947) Trans. Frances Frenaye
(180) *Ibid*
(181) Mussolini, *Fall of Mussolini—His own Story* (New York, 1948) Ed. Max Ascoli. Trans. Frances Frenaye
(182) Mussolini, *My Autobiography*, *op. cit.*
(183) Pini, *op. cit.*
(184) Barzini, *op. cit.*
(185) *Ibid*
(186) Fermi, *op. cit.*
(187) Pini, *op. cit.*
(188) *Ibid*
(189) *Ibid*

(190) Kemechey, *op. cit.*
(191) "Cassius", *op. cit.*
(192) *Ibid*
(193) Borgese, *Goliath—The march of Fascism* (London, 1938)
(194) "Cassius', *op. cit.*
(195) Delzell, *Mediterranean Fascism, op. cit.*
(196) Baskerville, *What Next O Duce* (London, 1937)
(197) Borgese, *op. cit.*
(198) Badoglio, *The War in Abyssinia* (London, (1937)
(199) *The Times* (5th September, 1935)
(200) *Ibid*
(201) Quoted in Fermi, *op. cit.*
(202) Barzini, *op. cit.*

(203) Pini, *op. cit.*
(204) The Ciano Diaries, *op. cit.*
(205) Mussolini, *The Fall of Mussolini, op. cit.*
(206) Delzell, *Mediterranean Fascism, op. cit.*
(207) Dollman, *op. cit.*
(208) Carter, *Italy Speaks* (London, 1947)
(209) Dollman, *op. cit.*
(210) Carter, *op. cit.*
(211) Caccia - Dominioni, *Alamein 1933–62* (London, 1966)
(212) *Ciano's Diaries 1939–43* (London, 1947) Ed. M. Muggeridge
(213) Luzzatto, *Unknown War in Italy* (London, 1946)

(214) *Ciano's Diaries* 1939-43, *op. cit.*
(215) Luzzatto, *op. cit.*
(216) *Ibid*
(217) Fermi, *op. cit.*
(218) Mussolini, *The Fall of Mussolini, op. cit.*
(219) *Ibid*
(220) Delzell, *Mussolini's Enemies, op. cit.*
(221) Luzzatto, *op. cit.*
(222) Ginzburg, *op. cit.*
(223) *Ibid*
(224) Luzzatto, *op. cit.*
(225) *Ibid*
(226) *Ibid*
(227) Barzini, *op. cit.*
(228) *Ibid*
(229) Mussolini, *The Fall of Mussolini, op. cit.*

Picture Credits

The Publishers wish to thank the following for their kind permission to reproduce copyright illustrations on the pages mentioned: the Radio Times Hulton Picture Library, 43, 44, 46, 48, 49, 53, 77, 99, 105; the Mansell Collection, *frontispiece*, 8, 17, 39, 41, 42, 45, 56, 94; Keystone Press Agency Ltd., 12, 16, 27, 32–33, 58–59, 60–61, 74–75, 91, 102–103, 108–109, 110, 111, 115 118; Moro, Rome, 15, 31, 47, 54, 70–71; Lords Gallery, 18, 25. The maps appearing on pages 11 and 97 are reproduced from Martin Gilbert's *Recent History Atlas* (1966) by the kind permission of the publishers Weidenfeld & Nicolson Ltd.

Further Reading

FOREIGN POLICY AND WAR

F. W. Deakin, *The Brutal Friendship* (London, Penguin, 1966; New York, Harper & Row, 1963)

Elizabeth Wiskemann, *The Rome-Berlin Axis* (London, Fontana, 1969; New York, O.U.P., 1949)

MUSSOLINI

Laura Fermi, *Mussolini* (London, University of Chicago Press, 1968; Chicago, University of Chicago Press, 1961)

Sir Ivone Kirkpatrick, *Mussolini: A Study in Power* (London, Odhams, 1964; New York, Hawthorne Books, 1964)

GENERAL

Luigi Barzini, *The Italians* (London, Hamish Hamilton, 1964; New York, Atheneum, 1964)

Alan Cassels, *Fascist Italy* (London, Routledge & Kegan Paul, 1969; New York, Thomas Crowell, 1969)

Cicely Hamilton, *Modern Italy* (London, Dent, 1932)

Dennis Mack Smith, *Italy—A Modern History* (London, Mayflower, 1959; Michigan, University of Michigan Press, 1959)

Index

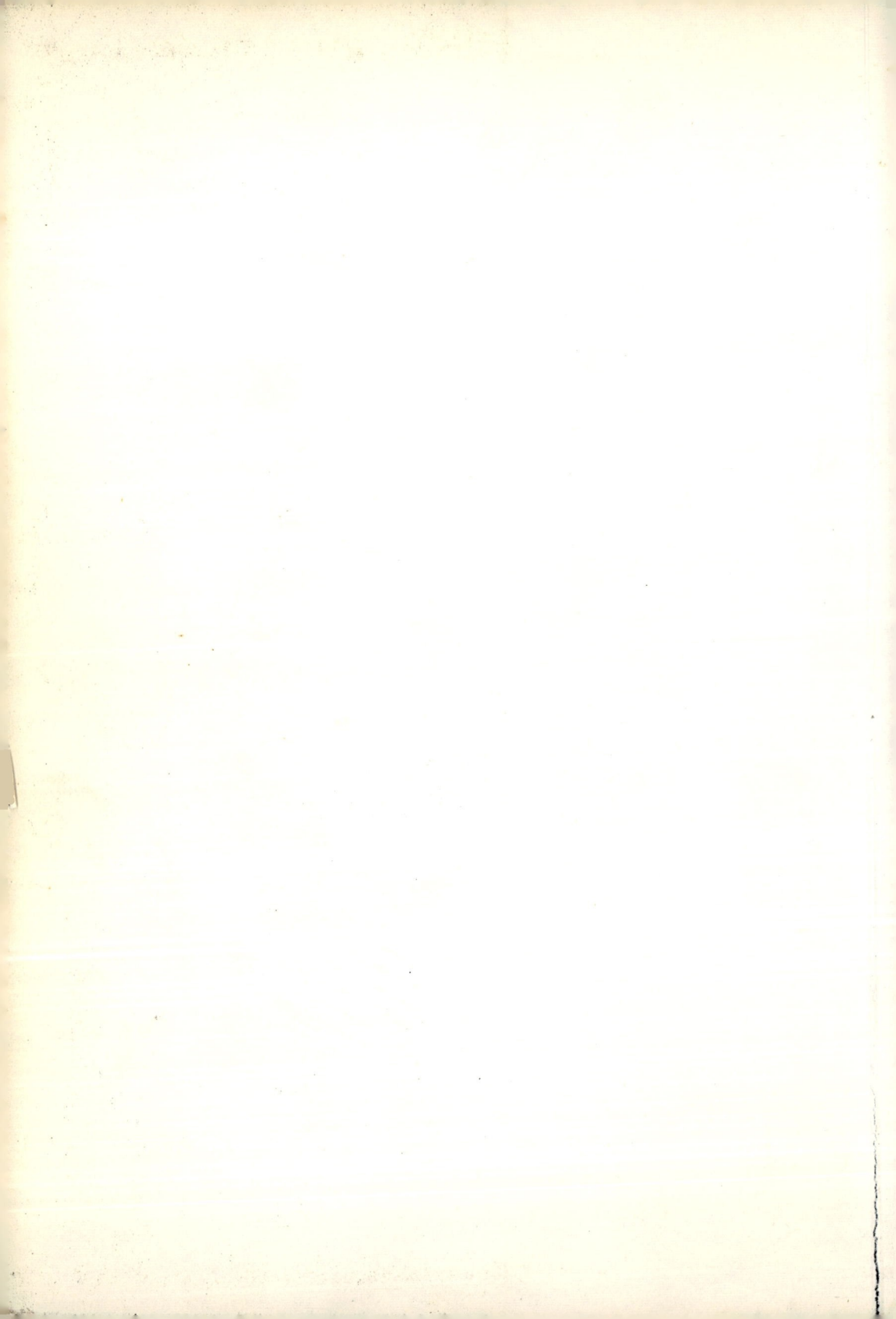